Peter Drucker

on the Profession of Management

Peter F. Drucker

A Harvard Business Review Book

The *Harvard Business Review* articles in this collection are available as individual reprints. Discounts apply to quantity purchases. For information and ordering contact Customer Service, Harvard Business School Publishing, Boston, MA 02163. Telephone: (617) 495-6192, 9 A.M. to 5 P.M. Eastern Time, Monday through Friday. Fax: (617) 495-6985, 24 hours a day.

Library of Congress Cataloging-in-Publication Data

Drucker, Peter Ferdinand, 1909-
    Peter Drucker on the profession of management / Peter F. Drucker.
      p.   cm. – (The Harvard Business Review book series)
    A collection of articles published in the Harvard Business Review between 1963-1994.
    Includes index.
    ISBN 0-87584-836-2 (alk. paper)
    1. Industrial management. I. Title. II. Title: Profession of Management   III. Series.
    HD31.D7742   1998
    658–dc21   97-39984
                                                            CIP

The paper used in this publication meets the requirements of the American National Standard for Permanence of Paper for Printed Library Materials Z39.48-1984.

Contents

Preface

The Future That Has Already Happened

In human affairs—political, social, economic, and business—it is pointless to try to predict the future, let alone attempt to look ahead 75 years. But it is possible—and fruitful—to identify major events that have already happened, irrevocably, and that therefore will have predictable effects in the next decade or two. It is possible, in other words, to identify and prepare for the future *that has already happened.*

The dominant factor for business in the next two decades—absent war, pestilence, or collision with a comet—is not going to be economics or technology. It will be demographics. The key factor for business will not be the *over*population of the world, of which we have been warned these last 40 years. It will be the increasing *under*population of the developed countries—Japan and those in Europe and in North America.

The developed world is in the process of committing collective national suicide. Its citizens are not producing enough babies to reproduce themselves, and the cause is quite clear. Its younger people are no longer able to bear the increasing burden of supporting a growing population of older, nonworking people. They can only offset that rising burden by cutting back at the other end of the dependence spectrum, which means having fewer or no children.

Of course, birthrates may go up again, though so far there is not the slightest sign of a new baby boom in any developed country. But even if birthrates increased overnight to the three-plus figure of the U.S. baby boom of 50 years ago, it would take 25 years before those new babies would become fully educated and productive adults. For the next 25 years, in other words, the underpopulation of the developed countries is accomplished fact and thus has the following implications for their societies and economies:

- Actual retirement age–the age at which people stop working–will go up in all developed countries to 75 for healthy people, who are the great majority. That rise in retirement age will occur well before the year 2010.

- Economic growth can no longer come from either putting more people to work–that is, from more resource input, as much of it has come in the past–nor from greater consumer demand. It can come only from a very sharp and continuing increase in the productivity of the one resource in which the developed countries still have an edge (and which they are likely to maintain for a few more decades): the productivity of knowledge work and of knowledge workers.

- There will be no single dominant world economic power, because no developed country has the population base to support such a role. There can be no long-term competitive advantage for any country, industry, or company, because neither money nor technology can, for any length of time, offset the growing imbalances in labor resources. The training methodologies developed during the two world wars–mostly in the U.S.–now make it possible to raise the productivity of a preindustrial and unskilled manual labor force to world-class levels in virtually no time, as Korea demonstrated 30 years ago and Thailand is demonstrating now. Technology–brand-new technology–is available, as a rule, quite cheaply on the open market. The only comparative advantage of the developed countries is in the supply of knowledge workers. It is not a qualitative advantage; the educated people in emerging countries are every whit as knowledgeable as their counterparts in the developed world. But quantitatively, the developed countries have an enormous lead. To convert this quantitative into a qualitative lead is one–and perhaps the only–way for the developed countries to maintain their competitive position in the world economy. This means continual, systematic work on the productivity of knowledge and knowledge workers, which is still neglected and abysmally low.

Knowledge is different from all other resources. It makes itself constantly obsolete, so that today's advanced knowledge is tomorrow's ignorance. And the knowledge that matters is subject to rapid and abrupt shifts—from pharmacology to genetics in the health care industry, for example, or from PCs to the Internet in the computer industry.

The productivity of knowledge and knowledge workers will not be the only competitive factor in the world economy. It is, however, likely to become the decisive factor, at least for most industries in the developed countries. The likelihood of this prediction holds implications for businesses and for executives.

- The first—and overarching—implication is that the world economy will continue to be highly turbulent and highly competitive, prone to abrupt shifts as both the nature and the content of relevant knowledge continually and unpredictably change.

- The information needs of businesses and of executives are likely to change rapidly. We have concentrated these past years on improving traditional information, which is almost exclusively information about what goes on *inside* an organization. Accounting, the traditional information system and the one on which most executives still depend, records what happens within the firm. All recent changes and improvements in accounting—such as activity-based accounting, the executive scorecard, and economic value analysis (EVA)—still aim at providing better information about events inside the company. The data produced by most new information systems also have that purpose. In fact, approximately 90 percent or more of the data any organization collects is information about inside events. Increasingly, a winning strategy will demand information about events and conditions *outside* the institution: noncustomers, technologies other than those currently used by the firm and its present competitors, markets not presently served, and so on. Only with this information can a business decide how to allocate its knowledge resources to produce the highest yield. Only with such information can a business also prepare for new changes and challenges arising from sudden shifts in the world economy and in the nature and the content of knowledge itself. The development of rigorous methods for gathering and analyzing outside information will increasingly become a major challenge for businesses and for information experts.

- Knowledge makes resources mobile. Knowledge workers, unlike manual workers in manufacturing, own the means of production: they carry that knowledge in their heads and can therefore take it with them. At the same time, the knowledge needs of organizations are likely to change continually. As a result, in developed countries more and more of the critical work force–and the most highly paid part of it–will increasingly consist of people who cannot be "managed" in the traditional sense of the word. In many cases, they will not even be employees of the organizations for which they work, but rather contractors, experts, consultants, part-timers, joint-venture partners, and so on. An increasing number of these people will identify themselves by their own knowledge rather than by the organization that pays them.

- Implicit in all this is a change in the very meaning of *organization*. For more than a century–from J. P. Morgan and John D. Rockefeller in the U.S., to George Siemens in Germany, to Henri Fayol in France, through Alfred Sloan at GM, and up to the present infatuation with teams–we have been searching for the one *right* organization for our companies. There can no longer be any such thing. There will be only "organizations"–as different from one other as a petroleum refinery, a cathedral, and a suburban bungalow are, even though all three are "buildings." Each organization in the developed countries (and not only businesses) will have to be designed for a specific task, time, and place (or culture).

- There are also implications for the art and science of management. Management will increasingly extend beyond business enterprises, where it originated some 125 years ago as an attempt to organize the production of *things*. The most important area for developing new concepts, methods, and practices will be in the management of society's *knowledge resources*–specifically, education and health care, both of which are today overadministered and undermanaged.

Predictions? No. These are the implications of a future *that has already happened.*

Introduction

Nan Stone

Management has become such a familiar and pervasive part of our lives that it is startling to realize that the field, as an object of study and as a profession, is so young. But in fact, when Peter Drucker began to study General Motors' policies and structure in 1943, he found (in his words) "pitifully few books and articles . . . in what we now call 'management'. " Those few that did exist dealt mostly with the specifics of factory operations or good salesmanship or the fine points of finance. Management as a concept had yet to be defined; "indeed most managers did not realize that they were practicing management."

Half a century later, the situation is markedly different. Volumes on management fill bookstores and library shelves. Business schools and MBAs have proliferated, not only in the United States but around the world. Executive education is a thriving business, as is management consulting. Management, in short, has become a well-established discipline; and the book that helped to launch this discipline was *The Concept of the Corporation,* the publication that emerged from Drucker's study of GM.

Drucker himself describes the timing of *The Concept of the Corporation* as largely a matter of luck: "I happened to be there first." But for Drucker, as for pioneers in every field, being there first required a great deal more than luck. Born in Vienna, Austria, in 1909, Drucker grew up surrounded by men and women who cared about politics and society, art and history. Educated classically and in the law, his real schooling came from the people he met and the work he undertook, first as a newspaper journalist and editor in Frankfurt, then as a merchant banker in London, and finally as a college teacher in the United States. The combination of these experiences brought him to the attention of GM's vice chairman, Donaldson Brown. Brown had read Drucker's *The Future of Industrial Man* and thought Drucker might be willing to spend some time inside GM, looking at the company from a social scientist's perspective. Even though Drucker knew that his choice of such an inappropriate subject as big business might damn him forever in the eyes of conventional academics, he was more than willing; he was enthusiastic. He had already concluded that the large business enterprise had become the most important institution in industrial society, and he wanted to understand how it worked.[1]

It is hard to imagine a more fruitful choice. *The Concept of the Corporation* proved to be only the first in a long line of his best-sellers on the practice of management and its role in modern society. Drucker has also had a long and distinguished career as a management professor, first at New York University's Graduate School of Business and, since 1971, at the Claremont Graduate School in California, which has named its management center in his honor. He has an unparalleled reputation as a counselor to senior managers: for more than 50 years, chief executives in companies around the globe have sought Drucker's advice—and taken it. So have leaders in government and the not-for-profit sector.

Peter's equally distinguished association with *Harvard Business Review* began in 1950 with "Management Must Manage" and continues to flourish today. His most recent article, "The Future That Has Already Happened," appears as the lead article in the special section commemorating the 75th anniversary of the *Harvard Business Review*. In the intervening years, Peter published more than 30 articles in the *Review*, six of which won McKinsey Awards.[2] No other *Harvard Business Review* author has been so remarkably productive or so unfailingly provocative.[3]

Although Peter clearly relishes the role of contrarian, the provocative quality of his writing owes less to the desire to shock than to certain habits of mind: in particular, the habit of looking hard at things as they are—not as they might be or are reputed to be—and then thinking hard about the implications. The preface to this collection, "The Future That Has Already Happened," provides a first-rate example of what I mean. When asked by *Harvard Business Review*'s editors what he thought the biggest challenge for management in the new century would be, Drucker neither cited the usual suspects (like technological change or globalization) nor engaged in speculation. Instead he pointed to a phenomenon previously noted only by demographers (the increasing under-population of the world's developed countries) and explained why–and how–it will affect both the competitive environment for business and the nature of management's most important tasks.

"The Coming of the New Organization," published in 1988, marked my first opportunity to work with Peter as his editor. This essay on the ways new information technology would transform not only the organization of work but the structure of organizations is characteristically prescient. Here Drucker anticipated many of the changes that took place in companies throughout the world during the 1990s, among them reengineering in the true sense of that word. So many of Peter's insights have become part of mainstream managerial thinking ten years later, it is almost impossible to appreciate how truly innovative they were.

Editing Peter presents a challenging, humbling, and enormously enjoyable task. His analyses always include something (or more often several somethings) that obliges the reader to abandon familiar explanations and entertain new concepts. The historical knowledge and moral imagination he brings to his writing are profound. Because Peter is, quite simply, one of the most direct, least pretentious people imaginable, working with him is a pleasure. He speaks his mind and expects the same of those around him. He welcomes questions. Above all, he recognizes and appreciates the contributions of others, whether well-known fellow management experts or anonymous members of an editorial staff.

I asked two simple questions when I chose the material for this collection: Was the article still fresh and relevant for a present-day reader? Could it stand on its own? Articles that required introductions to place them in context or notes to remind readers about pertinent historical events, though filled with sound advice and insight, didn't make the cut. My reasons for being so present-minded were many, not least of which was Peter's insistence that any collection we might publish be able to answer the reader's question, Why this book, now? Ultimately, I wanted to present Peter directly, in his own voice, and speaking to the important issues of the day–the same way he has always appeared in *Harvard Business Review*. This figured most prominently in my selection of articles for this collection.

The 13 chapters that ultimately emerged from this process divide into two distinct sections. The first, called "The Manager's Responsibilities," devotes itself to the fundamental work of management. While the earliest of the articles in this section, "Managing for Business Effectiveness," predates the most recent, "The Theory of the Business," by 30 years, both are concerned with the executive's most important task–the hard and risky work of ensuring the long-term health of the enterprise. Other recurrent topics in this section involve effective decision making, the systematic practice of innovation, and the responsible management of other people.

The second section, "The Executive's World," addresses the particular challenges of managing in a knowledge economy. Peter was among the first to observe the transformation of industrial economies into knowledge economies and to explore the implications of this change for the work of management. In fact, he began writing about the knowledge worker in 1969 when most, if not all, business writers were still focused on the productivity of manual workers. The motivation and organization of knowledge workers, the challenges of making service work productive, and the information that executives truly need to lead their organizations successfully are among the critical issues discussed.

At this point there is nothing left to say but "jump in." I hope you will enjoy reading this collection as much as I enjoyed assembling it.

Articles by Peter F. Drucker Appearing in *Harvard Business Review* from 1950 through 1995

"Management Must Manage," 28, no. 2 (1950)
"Population Trends and Management Policy," 29, no. 3 (1951)
"Basic Elements of a Free, Dynamic Society–Part I" (with Hoffman et al.), 29, no. 6 (1951)
"Basic Elements of a Free, Dynamic Society–Part II," 30, no. 1 (1952)

The Manager's Responsibilities

1 The Theory
of the Business

N OT in a very long time—not, perhaps, since the late 1940s or early 1950s—have there been as many new major management techniques as there are today: downsizing, outsourcing, total quality management, economic value analysis, benchmarking, reengineering. Each is a powerful tool. But, with the exceptions of outsourcing and reengineering, these tools are designed primarily to do differently what is already being done. They are "how to do" tools.

Yet "what to do" is increasingly becoming the central challenge facing managements, especially those of big companies that have enjoyed long-term success. The story is a familiar one: a company that was a superstar only yesterday finds itself stagnating and frustrated, in trouble and, often, in a seemingly unmanageable crisis. This phenomenon is by no means confined to the United States. It has become common in Japan and Germany, the Netherlands and France, Italy and Sweden. And it occurs just as often outside business—in labor unions, government agencies, hospitals, museums, and churches. In fact, it seems even less tractable in those areas.

The root cause of nearly every one of these crises is not that things are being done poorly. It is not even that the wrong things are being done. Indeed, in most cases, the *right* things are being done—but fruitlessly. What accounts for this apparent paradox? The assumptions on which the organization has been built and is being run no longer fit reality. These are the assumptions that shape any organiza-

September–October 1994

tion's behavior, dictate its decisions about what to do and what not to do, and define what the organization considers meaningful results. These assumptions are about markets. They are about identifying customers and competitors, their values and behavior. They are about technology and its dynamics, about a company's strengths and weaknesses. These assumptions are about what a company gets paid for. They are what I call a company's *theory of the business.*

Every organization, whether a business or not, has a theory of the business. Indeed, a valid theory that is clear, consistent, and focused is extraordinarily powerful. In 1809, for instance, German statesman and scholar Wilhelm von Humboldt founded the University of Berlin on a radically new theory of the university. And for more than 100 years, until the rise of Hitler, his theory defined the German university, especially in scholarship and scientific research. In 1870, Georg Siemens, the architect and first CEO of Deutsche Bank, the first universal bank, had an equally clear theory of the business: to use entrepreneurial finance to unify a still rural and splintered Germany through industrial development. Within 20 years of its founding, Deutsche Bank had become Europe's premier financial institution, which it has remained to this day in spite of two world wars, inflation, and Hitler. And, in the 1870s, Mitsubishi was founded on a clear and completely new theory of the business, which within 10 years made it the leader in an emerging Japan and within another 20 years made it one of the first truly multinational businesses.

Similarly, the theory of the business explains both the success of companies like General Motors and IBM, which have dominated the U.S. economy for the latter half of the twentieth century, and the challenges they have faced. In fact, what underlies the current malaise of so many large and successful organizations worldwide is that their theory of the business no longer works.

WHENEVER a big organization gets into trouble—and especially if it has been successful for many years—people blame sluggishness, complacency, arrogance, mammoth bureaucracies. A plausible explanation? Yes. But rarely the relevant or correct one. Consider the two most visible and widely reviled "arrogant bureaucracies" among large U.S. companies that have recently been in trouble.

Since the earliest days of the computer, it had been an article of faith at IBM that the computer would go the way of electricity. The future, IBM knew, and could prove with scientific rigor, lay with the central station, the ever-more-powerful mainframe into which a huge number of users could plug. Everything—economics, the logic of information, technology—led to that conclusion. But then, suddenly, when it seemed as if such a central-station, mainframe-based information system was actually coming into existence, two young men came up with the first personal computer. Every computer maker knew that the PC was absurd. It did not have the memory, the database, the speed, or the computing ability necessary to succeed. Indeed, every computer maker knew that the PC had to fail—the conclusion reached by Xerox only a few years earlier, when its research team had actually built the first PC. But when that misbegotten monstrosity—first the Apple, then the Macintosh—came on the market, people not only loved it, they bought it.

Every big, successful company throughout history, when confronted with such a surprise, has refused to accept it. "It's a stupid fad and will be gone in three years," said the CEO of Zeiss upon seeing the new Kodak Brownie in 1888, when the German company was as dominant in the world photographic market as IBM would be in the computer market a century later. Most mainframe makers responded in the same way. The list was long: Control Data, Univac, Burroughs, and NCR in the United States; Siemens, Nixdorf, Machines Bull, and ICL in Europe; Hitachi and Fujitsu in Japan. IBM, the overlord of mainframes with as much in sales as all the other computer makers put together and with record profits, could have reacted in the same way. In fact, it *should* have. Instead, IBM immediately accepted the PC as the new reality. Almost overnight, it brushed aside all its proven and time-tested policies, rules, and regulations and set up not one but two competing teams to design an even simpler PC. A couple of years later, IBM had become the world's largest PC manufacturer and the industry standard setter.

There is absolutely no precedent for this achievement in all of business history; it hardly argues bureaucracy, sluggishness, or arrogance. Yet despite unprecedented flexibility, agility, and humility, IBM was floundering a few years later in both the mainframe and the PC business. It was suddenly unable to move, to take decisive action, to change.

The case of GM is equally perplexing. In the early 1980s–the very years in which GM's main business, passenger automobiles, seemed almost paralyzed–the company acquired two large businesses: Hughes Electronics and Ross Perot's Electronic Data Systems. Analysts generally considered both companies to be mature and chided GM for grossly overpaying for them. Yet, within a few short years, GM had more than tripled the revenues and profits of the allegedly mature EDS. And ten years later, in 1994, EDS had a market value six times the amount that GM had paid for it and ten times its original revenues and profits.

Similarly, GM bought Hughes Electronics–a huge but profitless company involved exclusively in defense–just before the defense industry collapsed. Under GM management, Hughes has actually increased its defense profits and has become the only big defense contractor to move successfully into large-scale nondefense work. Remarkably, the same bean counters who had been so ineffectual in the automobile business–30-year GM veterans who had never worked for any other company or, for that matter, outside of finance and accounting departments–were the ones who achieved those startling results. And in the two acquisitions, they simply applied policies, practices, and procedures that had already been used by GM.

This story is a familiar one at GM. Since the company's founding in a flurry of acquisitions 80 years ago, one of its core competencies has been to "overpay" for well-performing but mature businesses–as it did for Buick, AC Spark Plug, and Fisher Body in those early years–and then turn them into world-class champions. Very few companies have been able to match GM's performance in making successful acquisitions, and GM surely did not accomplish those feats by being bureaucratic, sluggish, or arrogant. Yet what worked so beautifully in those businesses that GM knew nothing about failed miserably in GM itself.

WHAT can explain the fact that at both IBM and GM the policies, practices, and behaviors that worked for decades–and in the case of GM are still working well when applied to something new and different–no longer work for the organization in which and for which they were developed? The realities that each organization actually faces have changed quite dramatically from those that each still assumes it lives with. Put another way, reality has changed, but the theory of the business has not changed with it.

Before its agile response to the new reality of the PC, IBM had once before turned its basic strategy around overnight. In 1950, Univac, then the world's leading computer company, showed the prototype of the first machine designed to be a multipurpose computer. All earlier designs had been for single-purpose machines. IBM's own two earlier computers, built in the late 1930s and 1946, respectively, performed astronomical calculations only. And the machine that IBM had on the drawing board in 1950, intended for the SAGE air defense system in the Canadian Arctic, had only one purpose: early identification of enemy aircraft. IBM immediately scrapped its strategy of developing advanced single-purpose machines; it put its best engineers to work on perfecting the Univac architecture and, from it, designing the first multipurpose computer able to be manufactured (rather than handcrafted) and serviced. Three years later, IBM had become the world's dominant computer maker and standard-bearer. IBM did not create the computer. But in 1950, its flexibility, speed, and humility created the computer *industry.*

However, the same assumptions that had helped IBM prevail in 1950 proved to be its undoing 30 years later. In the 1970s, IBM assumed that there was such a thing as a "computer," just as it had in the 1950s. But the emergence of the PC invalidated that assumption. Mainframe computers and PCs are, in fact, no more one entity than are generating stations and electric toasters. The latter, while different, are interdependent and complementary. In contrast, mainframe computers and PCs are primarily competitors. And, in their basic definition of *information,* they actually contradict each other: for the mainframe, information means memory; for the brainless PC, it means software. Building generating stations and making toasters must be run as separate businesses, but they can be owned by the same corporate entity, as General Electric did for decades. In contrast, mainframe computers and PCs probably cannot coexist in the same corporate entity.

IBM tried to combine the two. But because the PC was the fastest growing part of the business, IBM could not subordinate it to the mainframe business. As a result, the company could not optimize the mainframe business. And because the mainframe was still the cash cow, IBM could not optimize the PC business. In the end, the assumption that a computer is a computer–or, more prosaically, that the industry is hardware driven–paralyzed IBM.

GM had an even more powerful, and successful, theory of the business than IBM had, one that made GM the world's largest and most profitable manufacturing organization. The company did not have one setback in 70 years–a record unmatched in business history. GM's theory combined in one seamless web assumptions about markets and customers with assumptions about core competencies and organizational structure.

Since the early 1920s, GM assumed that the U.S. automobile market was homogeneous in its values and segmented by extremely stable income groups. The resale value of the "good" used car was the only independent variable under management's control. High trade-in values enabled customers to upgrade their new-car purchases to the next category–in other words, to cars with higher profit margins. According to this theory, frequent or radical changes in models could only depress trade-in values.

Internally, these market assumptions went hand in hand with assumptions about how production should be organized to yield the biggest market share and the highest profit. In GM's case, the answer was long runs of mass-produced cars with a minimum of changes each model year, resulting in the largest number of uniform yearly models on the market at the lowest fixed cost per car.

GM's management then translated these assumptions about market and production into a structure of semiautonomous divisions, each focusing on one income segment and each arranged so that its highest priced model overlapped with the next division's lowest priced model, thus almost forcing people to trade up, provided that used-car prices were high.

For 70 years, this theory worked like a charm. Even in the depths of the Depression, GM never suffered a loss while steadily gaining market share. But in the late 1970s, its assumptions about the market and about production became invalid. The market was fragmenting into highly volatile "lifestyle" segments. Income became one factor among many in the buying decision, not the only one. At the same time, lean manufacturing created an economics of small scale. It made short runs and variations in models less costly and more profitable than long runs of uniform products.

GM knew all this but simply could not believe it. (GM's union still doesn't.) Instead, the company tried to patch things over. It maintained the existing divisions based on income segmentation, but each division now offered a "car for every purse." It tried to compete with lean manufacturing's economics of small scale by automating the large-scale, long-run mass production (losing some $30 billion in the process). Contrary to popular belief, GM patched things over with prodigious energy, hard work, and lavish investments of time and money. But patching only confused the customer, the dealer, and the employees and management of GM itself. In the meantime, GM neglected its *real* growth market, where it had leadership and would have been almost unbeatable: light trucks and minivans.

A THEORY of the business has three parts. First, there are assumptions about the environment of the organization: society and its structure, the market, the customer, and technology.

Second, there are assumptions about the specific mission of the organization. Sears, Roebuck and Company, in the years during and following World War I, defined its mission as being the informed buyer for the American family. A decade later, Marks and Spencer in Great Britain defined its mission as being the change agent in British society by becoming the first classless retailer. AT&T, again in the years during and immediately after World War I, defined its role as ensuring that every U.S. family and business have access to a telephone. An organization's mission need not be so ambitious. GM envisioned a far more modest role—as the leader in "terrestrial motorized transportation equipment," in the words of Alfred P. Sloan, Jr.

Third, there are assumptions about the core competencies needed to accomplish the organization's mission. For example, West Point, founded in 1802, defined its core competence as the ability to turn out leaders who deserve trust. Marks and Spencer, around 1930, defined its core competence as the ability to identify, design, and develop the merchandise it sold, instead of as the ability to buy. AT&T, around 1920, defined its core competence as technical leadership that would enable the company to improve service continuously while steadily lowering rates.

The assumptions about environment define what an organization is paid for. The assumptions about mission define what an organization considers to be meaningful results; in other words, they point to how it envisions itself making a difference in the economy and in the society at large. Finally, the assumptions about core competencies define where an organization must excel in order to maintain leadership.

Of course, all this sounds deceptively simple. It usually takes years of hard work, thinking, and experimenting to reach a clear, consistent, and valid theory of the business. Yet to be successful, every organization must work one out.

What are the specifications of a valid theory of the business? There are four.

1. *The assumptions about environment, mission, and core competencies must fit reality.* When four penniless young men from Manchester, England, Simon Marks and his three brothers-in-law, decided in the early 1920s that a humdrum penny bazaar should become an agent of social change, World War I had profoundly shaken their country's class structure. It had also created masses of new buyers for good-quality, stylish, but cheap merchandise like lingerie, blouses, and stockings—Marks and Spencer's first successful product categories. Marks and Spencer then systematically set to work developing brand-new and unheard-of core competencies. Until then, the core competence of a merchant was the ability to buy well. Marks and Spencer decided that it was the merchant, rather than the manufacturer, who knew the customer. Therefore, the merchant, not the manufacturer, should design the products, develop them, and find producers to make the goods to

his design, specifications, and costs. This new definition of the merchant took five to eight years to develop and make acceptable to traditional suppliers, who had always seen themselves as "manufacturers," not "subcontractors."

2. *The assumptions in all three areas have to fit one another.* This was perhaps GM's greatest strength in the long decades of its ascendancy. Its assumptions about the market and about the optimum manufacturing process were a perfect fit. GM decided in the mid-1920s that it also required new and as-yet-unheard-of core competencies: financial control of the manufacturing process and a theory of capital allocations. As a result, GM invented modern cost accounting and the first rational capital-allocation process.

3. *The theory of the business must be known and understood throughout the organization.* That is easy in an organization's early days. But as it becomes successful, an organization tends increasingly to take its theory for granted, becoming less and less conscious of it. Then the organization becomes sloppy. It begins to cut corners. It begins to pursue what is expedient rather than what is right. It stops thinking. It stops questioning. It remembers the answers but has forgotten the questions. The theory of the business becomes "culture." But culture is no substitute for discipline, and the theory of the business is a discipline.

4. *The theory of the business has to be tested constantly.* It is not graven on tablets of stone. It is a hypothesis. And it is a hypothesis about things that are in constant flux—society, markets, customers, technology. And so, built into the theory of the business must be the ability to change itself.

S O M E theories of the business are so powerful that they last for a long time. But being human artifacts, they don't last forever, and, indeed, today they rarely last for very long at all. Eventually every theory of the business becomes obsolete and then invalid. That is precisely what happened to those on which the great U.S. businesses of the 1920s were built. It happened to the GMs and the AT&Ts. It has happened to IBM. It is clearly happening today to Deutsche Bank and its theory of the universal bank. It is also clearly happening to the rapidly unraveling Japanese *keiretsu.*

The first reaction of an organization whose theory is becoming obsolete is almost always a defensive one. The tendency is to put one's head in the sand and pretend that nothing is happening. The next reaction is an attempt to patch, as GM did in the early 1980s or as Deutsche Bank is doing today. Indeed, the sudden and completely unexpected crisis of one big German company after another for which Deutsche Bank is the "house bank" indicates that its theory no longer works. That is, Deutsche Bank no longer does what it was designed to do: provide effective governance of the modern corporation.

But patching never works. Instead, when a theory shows the first signs of becoming obsolete, it is time to start thinking again, to ask again which assumptions about the environment, mission, and core competencies reflect reality most accurately–with the clear premise that our historically transmitted assumptions, those with which all of us grew up, no longer suffice.

WHAT, then, needs to be done? There is a need for preventive care–that is, for building into the organization systematic monitoring and testing of its theory of the business. There is a need for early diagnosis. Finally, there is a need to rethink a theory that is stagnating and to take effective action in order to change policies and practices, bringing the organization's behavior in line with the new realities of its environment, with a new definition of its mission, and with new core competencies to be developed and acquired.

Preventive Care

There are only two preventive measures. But, if used consistently, they should keep an organization alert and capable of rapidly changing itself and its theory. The first measure is what I call *abandonment*. Every three years, an organization should challenge every product, every service, every policy, every distribution channel with the question, If we were not in it already, would we be going into it now? By questioning accepted policies and routines, the organization forces itself to think about its theory. It forces itself to test assumptions. It forces itself to ask: Why didn't this work, even though it looked so promising when we went into it five years ago? Is it because we made a mistake? Is it because we did the wrong things? Or is it because the right things didn't work?

Without systematic and purposeful abandonment, an organization will be overtaken by events. It will squander its best resources on things it should never have been doing or should no longer do. As a result, it will lack the resources, especially capable people, needed to exploit the opportunities that arise when markets, technologies, and core competencies change. In other words, it will be unable to respond constructively to the opportunities that are created when its theory of the business becomes obsolete.

The second preventive measure is to study what goes on outside the business, and especially to study *noncustomers*. Walk-around management became fashionable a few years back. It *is* important. And so is knowing as much as possible about one's customers—the area, perhaps, where information technology is making the most rapid advances. But the first signs of fundamental change rarely appear within one's own organization or among one's own customers. Almost always they show up first among one's noncustomers. Noncustomers always outnumber customers. Wal-Mart, today's retail giant, has 14 percent of the U.S. consumer-goods market. That means 86 percent of the market is noncustomers.

In fact, the best recent example of the importance of the noncustomer is U.S. department stores. At their peak some 20 years ago, department stores served 30 percent of the U.S. nonfood retail market. They questioned their customers constantly, studied them, surveyed them. But they paid no attention to the 70 percent of the market who were not their customers. They saw no reason why they should. Their theory of the business assumed that most people who could afford to shop in department stores did. Fifty years ago, that assumption fit reality. But when the baby boomers came of age, it ceased to be valid. For the dominant group among baby boomers—women in educated two-income families—it was not money that determined where to shop. Time was the primary factor, and this generation's women could not afford to spend their time shopping in department stores. Because department stores looked only at their own customers, they did not recognize this change until a few years ago. By then, business was already drying up. And it was too late to get the baby boomers back. The department stores learned the hard way that although being customer driven is vital, it is not enough. An organization must be market driven too.

Early Diagnosis

To diagnose problems early, managers must pay attention to the warning signs. A theory of the business always becomes obsolete when an organization attains its original objectives. Attaining one's objectives, then, is not cause for celebration; it is cause for new thinking. AT&T accomplished its mission to give every U.S. family and business access to the telephone by the mid-1950s. Some executives then said it was time to reassess the theory of the business and, for instance, separate local service–where the objectives had been reached–from growing and future businesses, beginning with long-distance service and extending into global telecommunications. Their arguments went unheeded, and a few years later AT&T began to flounder, only to be rescued by antitrust, which did by fiat what the company's management had refused to do voluntarily.

Rapid growth is another sure sign of crisis in an organization's theory. Any organization that doubles or triples in size within a fairly short period of time has necessarily outgrown its theory. Even Silicon Valley has learned that beer bashes are no longer adequate for communication once a company has grown so big that people have to wear name tags. But such growth challenges much deeper assumptions, policies, and habits. To continue in health, let alone grow, the organization has to ask itself again the questions about its environment, mission, and core competencies.

There are two more clear signals that an organization's theory of the business is no longer valid. One is unexpected success–whether one's own or a competitor's. The other is unexpected failure–again, whether one's own or a competitor's.

At the same time that Japanese automobile imports had Detroit's Big Three on the ropes, Chrysler registered a totally unexpected success. Its traditional passenger cars were losing market share even faster than GM's and Ford's were. But sales of its Jeep and its new minivans–an almost accidental development–skyrocketed. At the time, GM was the leader of the U.S. light-truck market and unchallenged in the design and quality of its products, but it wasn't paying any attention to its light-truck capacity. After all, minivans and light trucks had always been classified as commercial rather than passenger vehicles in traditional statistics, even though most of them are now being bought as passenger vehicles. However, had it paid attention to the success of its weaker competitor, Chrysler, GM might have realized much earlier that its assumptions about both its market and its core competencies were no longer valid. From the beginning, the minivan and light-truck market was not an income-class market and was little influenced by trade-in prices. And, paradoxically, light trucks were the one area in which GM, 15 years ago, had already moved quite far toward what we now call lean manufacturing.

Unexpected failure is as much a warning as unexpected success and should be taken as seriously as a 60-year-old man's first "minor" heart attack. Sixty years ago, in the midst of the Depression, Sears decided that automobile insurance had become an "accessory" rather than a financial product and that selling it would therefore fit its mission as being the informed buyer for the American family. Everyone thought Sears was crazy. But automobile insurance became Sears's most profitable business almost instantly. Twenty years later, in the 1950s, Sears decided that diamond rings had become a necessity rather than a luxury, and the company became the world's largest–and probably most profitable–diamond retailer. It was only logical for Sears to decide in 1981 that investment products had become consumer goods for the American family. It bought Dean Witter and moved its offices into Sears stores. The move was a total disaster. The U.S. public clearly did not consider its financial needs to be "consumer products." When Sears finally gave up and decided to run Dean Witter as a separate business outside Sears stores, Dean Witter at once began to blossom. In 1992, Sears sold it at a tidy profit.

Had Sears seen its failure to become the American family's supplier of investments as a failure of its theory and not as an isolated incident, it might have begun to restructure and reposition itself ten years earlier than it actually did, when it still had substantial market leadership. For Sears might then have seen, as several of its competitors like J.C. Penney immediately did, that the Dean Witter failure threw into doubt the entire concept of market homogeneity–the very concept on which Sears and other mass retailers had based their strategy for years.

Cure

Traditionally, we have searched for the miracle worker with a magic wand to turn an ailing organization around. To establish, maintain, and restore a theory, however, does not require a Genghis Khan or a Leonardo da Vinci in the executive suite. It is not genius; it is hard work. It is not being clever; it is being conscientious. It is what CEOs are paid for.

There are indeed quite a few CEOs who have successfully changed their theory of the business. The CEO who built Merck into the world's most successful pharmaceutical business by focusing solely on the research and development of patented, high-margin break-through drugs radically changed the company's theory by acquiring a large distributor of generic and nonprescription drugs. He did so without a "crisis," while Merck was ostensibly doing very well. Similarly, a few years ago, the new CEO of Sony, the world's best-known manufacturer of consumer electronic hardware, changed the company's theory of the business. He acquired a Hollywood movie production company and, with that acquisition, shifted the organization's center of gravity from being a hardware manufac-turer in search of software to being a software producer that creates a market demand for hardware.

But for every one of these apparent miracle workers, there are scores of equally capable CEOs whose organizations stumble. We can't rely on miracle workers to rejuvenate an obsolete theory of the business any more than we can rely on them to cure other types of serious illness. And when one talks to these supposed miracle workers, they deny vehemently that they act by charisma, vision, or, for that matter, the laying on of hands. They start out with diagno-sis and analysis. They accept that attaining objectives and rapid growth demand a serious rethinking of the theory of the business. They do not dismiss unexpected failure as the result of a subordi-nate's incompetence or as an accident but treat it as a symptom of "systems failure." They do not take credit for unexpected success but treat it as a challenge to their assumptions.

They accept that a theory's obsolescence is a degenerative and, indeed, life-threatening disease. And they know and accept the surgeon's time-tested principle, the oldest principle of effective decision making: A degenerative disease will not be cured by procrastination. It requires decisive action.

2   The Effective
Decision

E FFECTIVE executives do not make a great many decisions. They concentrate on what is important. They try to make the few important decisions on the highest level of conceptual understanding. They try to find the constants in a situation, to think through what is strategic and generic rather than to "solve problems." They are, therefore, not overly impressed by speed in decision making; rather, they consider virtuosity in manipulating a great many variables a symptom of sloppy thinking. They want to know what the decision is all about and what the underlying realities are which it has to satisfy. They want impact rather than technique. And they want to be sound rather than clever.

Effective executives know when a decision has to be based on principle and when it should be made pragmatically, on the merits of the case. They know the trickiest decision is that between the right and the wrong compromise, and they have learned to tell one from the other. They know that the most time-consuming step in the process is not making the decision but putting it into effect. Unless a decision has degenerated into work, it is not a decision; it is at best a good intention. This means that, while the effective decision itself is based on the highest level of conceptual understanding, the action commitment should be as close as possible to the capacities of the people who have to carry it out. Above all, effective

January–February 1967

executives know that decision making has its own systematic process and its own clearly defined elements.

Sequential Steps

The elements do not by themselves "make" the decisions. Indeed, every decision is a risk-taking judgment. But unless these elements are the stepping stones of the decision process, the executive will not arrive at a right, and certainly not at an effective, decision. Therefore, in this chapter I shall describe the sequence of steps involved in the decision-making process.

1. *Classifying the problem.* Is it generic? Is it exceptional and unique? Or is it the first manifestation of a new genus for which a rule has yet to be developed?

2. *Defining the problem.* What are we dealing with?

3. *Specifying the answer to the problem.* What are the "boundary conditions"?

4. *Deciding what is "right," rather than what is acceptable, in order to meet the boundary conditions.* What will fully satisfy the specifications *before* attention is given to the compromises, adaptations, and concessions needed to make the decision acceptable?

5. *Building into the decision the action to carry it out.* What does the action commitment have to be? Who has to know about it?

6. *Testing the validity and effectiveness of the decision against the actual course of events.* How is the decision being carried out? Are the assumptions on which it is based appropriate or obsolete?

Let us take a look at each of these individual elements.

The Classification

The effective decision maker asks: Is this a symptom of a fundamental disorder or a stray event? The generic always has to be answered through a rule, a principle. But the truly exceptional event can only be handled as such and as it comes.

Strictly speaking, the executive might distinguish among four, rather than between two, different types of occurrences.

First, there is the truly generic event, of which the individual occurrence is only a symptom. Most of the "problems" that come up in the course of the executive's work are of this nature. Inventory decisions in a business, for instance, are not "decisions." They are adaptations. The problem is generic. This is even more likely to be true of occurrences within manufacturing organizations. For example:

> A product control and engineering group will typically handle many hundreds of problems in the course of a month. Yet, whenever these are analyzed, the great majority prove to be just symptoms—and manifestations—of underlying basic situations. The individual process control engineer or production engineer who works in one part of the plant usually cannot see this. He might have a few problems each month with the couplings in the pipes that carry steam or hot liquids, and that's all.

Only when the total workload of the group over several months is analyzed does the generic problem appear. Then it is seen that temperatures or pressures have become too great for the existing equipment and that the couplings holding the various lines together need to be redesigned for greater loads. Until this analysis is done, process control will spend a tremendous amount of time fixing leaks without ever getting control of the situation.

The second type of occurrence is the problem which, while a unique event for the individual institution, is actually generic. Consider:

> The company that receives an offer to merge from another, larger one, will never receive such an offer again if it accepts. This is a nonrecurrent situation as far as the individual company, its board of directors, and its management are concerned. But it is, of course, a generic situation which occurs all the time. Thinking through whether to accept or to reject the offer requires some general rules. For these, however, the executive has to look to the experience of others.

Next there is the truly exceptional event that the executive must distinguish. To illustrate:

> The huge power failure that plunged into darkness the whole of Northeastern North America from St. Lawrence to Washington in November 1965 was, according to first explanations, a truly excep-

tional situation. So was the thalidomide tragedy which led to the birth of so many deformed babies in the early 1960s. The probability of either of these events occurring, we were told, was one in ten million or one in a hundred million, and concatenations of these events were as unlikely ever to recur again as it is unlikely, for instance, for the chair on which I sit to disintegrate into its constituent atoms.

Truly unique events are rare, however. Whenever one appears, the decision maker has to ask: Is this a true exception or only the first manifestation of a new genus? And this–the early manifestation of a new generic problem–is the fourth and last category of events with which the decision process deals. Thus:

> We know now that both the Northeastern power failure and the thalidomide tragedy were only the first occurrences of what, under conditions of modern power technology or of modern pharmacology, are likely to become fairly frequent occurrences unless generic solutions are found.

All events but the truly unique require a generic solution. They require a rule, a policy, or a principle. Once the right principle has been developed, all manifestations of the same generic situation can be handled pragmatically–that is, by adaptation of the rule to the concrete circumstances of the case. Truly unique events, however, must be treated individually. The executive cannot develop rules for the exceptional.

The effective decision maker spends time determining which of the four different situations is happening. The wrong decision will be made if the situation is classified incorrectly.

By far the most common mistake of the decision maker is to treat a generic situation as if it were a series of unique events–that is, to be pragmatic when lacking the generic understanding and principle. The inevitable result is frustration and futility. This was clearly shown, I think, by the failure of most of the policies, both domestic and foreign, of the Kennedy Administration. Consider:

> For all the brilliance of its members, the Administration achieved fundamentally only one success, and that was in the Cuban missile crisis. Otherwise, it achieved practically nothing. The main reason

was surely what its members called "pragmatism"–namely, the Administration's refusal to develop rules and principles, and its insistence on treating everything "on its merits." Yet it was clear to everyone, including the members of the Administration, that the basic assumptions on which its policies rested–the valid assumptions of the immediate postwar years–had become increasingly unrealistic in international, as well as in domestic, affairs in the 1960's.

Equally common is the mistake of treating a new event as if it were just another example of the old problem to which, therefore, the old rules should be applied:

> This was the error that snowballed the local power failure on the New York–Ontario border into the great Northeastern blackout. The power engineers, especially in New York City, applied the right rule for a normal overload. Yet their own instruments had signaled that something quite extraordinary was going on which called for exceptional, rather than standard, countermeasures.

By contrast, the one great triumph of President Kennedy in the Cuban missile crisis rested on acceptance of the challenge to think through an extraordinary, exceptional occurrence. As soon as he accepted this, his own tremendous resources of intelligence and courage effectively came into play.

The Definition

Once a problem has been classified as generic or unique, it is usually fairly easy to define. "What is this all about?" "What is pertinent here?" "What is the key to this situation?" Questions such as these are familiar. But only the truly effective decision makers are aware that the danger in this step is not the wrong definition; it is the plausible but incomplete one. For example:

> The American automobile industry held to a plausible but incomplete definition of the problem of automotive safety. It was this lack of awareness–far more than any reluctance to spend money on safety engineering–that eventually, in 1966, brought the industry under sudden and sharp Congressional attack for its unsafe cars

and then left the industry totally bewildered by the attack. It simply is not true that the industry has paid scant attention to safety.

On the contrary, it has worked hard at safer highway engineering and at driver training, believing these to be the major areas for concern. That accidents are caused by unsafe roads and unsafe drivers is plausible enough. Indeed, all other agencies concerned with automotive safety, from the highway police to the high schools, picked the same targets for their campaigns. These campaigns have produced results. The number of accidents on highways built for safety has been greatly lessened. Similarly, safety-trained drivers have been involved in far fewer accidents.

But although the ratio of accidents per thousand cars or per thousand miles driven has been going down, the total number of accidents and the severity of them have kept creeping up. It should therefore have become clear long ago that something would have to be done about the small but significant probability that accidents will occur despite safety laws and safety training.

This means that future safety campaigns will have to be supplemented by engineering to make accidents themselves less dangerous. Whereas cars have been engineered to be safe when used correctly, they will also have to be engineered for safety when used incorrectly.

There is only one safeguard against becoming the prisoner of an incomplete definition: check it again and again against *all* the observable facts, and throw out a definition the moment it fails to encompass any of them.

Effective decision makers always test for signs that something is atypical or something unusual is happening, always asking: Does the definition explain the observed events, and does it explain all of them? They always write out what the definition is expected to make happen—for instance, make automobile accidents disappear—and then test regularly to see if this really happens. Finally, they go back and think the problem through again whenever they see something atypical, when they find unexplained phenomena, or when the course of events deviates, even in details, from expectations.

These are in essence the rules Hippocrates laid down for medical diagnosis well over 2,000 years ago. They are the rules for scientific observation first formulated by Aristotle and then reaffirmed by

Galileo 300 years ago. These, in other words, are old, well-known, time-tested rules, which an executive can learn and apply systematically.

The Specifications

The next major element in the decision process is defining clear specifications as to what the decision has to accomplish. What are the objectives the decision has to reach? What are the minimum goals it has to attain? What are the conditions it has to satisfy? In science these are known as "boundary conditions." A decision, to be effective, needs to satisfy the boundary conditions. Consider:

"Can our needs be satisfied," Alfred P. Sloan, Jr. presumably asked himself when he took command of General Motors in 1922, "by removing the autonomy of our division heads?" His answer was clearly in the negative. The boundary conditions of his problem demanded strength and responsibility in the chief operating positions. This was needed as much as unity and control at the center. Everyone before Sloan had seen the problem as one of personalities—to be solved through a struggle for power from which one man would emerge victorious. The boundary conditions, Sloan realized, demanded a solution to a constitutional problem—to be solved through a new structure: decentralization which balanced local autonomy of operations with central control of direction and policy.

A decision that does not satisfy the boundary conditions is worse than one which wrongly defines the problem. It is all but impossible to salvage the decision that starts with the right premises but stops short of the right conclusions. Furthermore, clear thinking about the boundary conditions is needed to know when a decision has to be abandoned. The most common cause of failure in a decision lies not in its being wrong initially. Rather, it is a subsequent shift in the goals—the specifications—which makes the prior right decision suddenly inappropriate. And unless the decision maker has kept the boundary conditions clear, so as to make possible the immediate replacement of the outflanked decision with a new and appropriate policy, he may not even notice that things have changed. For example:

Franklin D. Roosevelt was bitterly attacked for his switch from conservative candidate in 1932 to radical president in 1933. But it wasn't Roosevelt who changed. The sudden economic collapse which occurred between the summer of 1932 and the spring of 1933 changed the specifications. A policy appropriate to the goal of national economic recovery—which a conservative economic policy might have been—was no longer appropriate when, with the Bank Holiday, the goal had to become political and social cohesion. When the boundary conditions changed, Roosevelt immediately substituted a political objective (reform) for his former economic one (recovery).

Above all, clear thinking about the boundary conditions is needed to identify the most dangerous of all possible decisions: the one in which the specifications that have to be satisfied are essentially incompatible. In other words, this is the decision that might—just might—work if nothing whatever goes wrong. A classic case is President Kennedy's Bay of Pigs decision:

> One specification was clearly Castro's overthrow. The other was to make it appear that the invasion was a "spontaneous" uprising of the Cubans. But these two specifications would have been compatible with each other only if an immediate island-wide uprising against Castro would have completely paralyzed the Cuban army. And while this was not impossible, it clearly was not probable in such a tightly controlled police state.

Decisions of this sort are usually called "gambles." But actually they arise from something much less rational than a gamble—namely, a hope against hope that two (or more) clearly incompatible specifications can be fulfilled simultaneously. This is hoping for a miracle; and the trouble with miracles is not that they happen so rarely, but that they are, alas, singularly unreliable.

Everyone can make the wrong decision. In fact, everyone will sometimes make a wrong decision. But no executive needs to make a decision which, on the face of it, seems to make sense but, in reality, falls short of satisfying the boundary conditions.

The Decision

The effective executive has to start out with what is "right" rather than what is acceptable precisely because a compromise is always necessary in the end. But if what will satisfy the boundary conditions is not known, the decision maker cannot distinguish between the right compromise and the wrong compromise–and may end up by making the wrong compromise. Consider:

> I was taught this lesson in 1944 when I started on my first big consulting assignment. It was a study of the management structure and policies of General Motors Corporation. Alfred P. Sloan, Jr., who was then chairman and chief executive officer of the company, called me to his office at the start of my assignment and said: "I shall not tell you what to study, what to write, or what conclusions to come to. This is your task. My only instruction to you is to put down what you think is right as you see it. Don't you worry about our reaction. Don't you worry about whether we will like this or dislike that. And don't you, above all, concern yourself with the compromises that might be needed to make your conclusions acceptable. There is not one executive in this company who does not know how to make every single conceivable compromise without any help from you. But he can't make the right compromise unless you first tell him what *right* is."

The effective executive knows that there are two different kinds of compromise. One is expressed in the old proverb, "Half a loaf is better than no bread." The other, in the story of the judgment of Solomon, is clearly based on the realization that "half a baby is worse than no baby at all." In the first instance, the boundary conditions are still being satisfied. The purpose of bread is to provide food, and half a loaf is still food. Half a baby, however, does not satisfy the boundary conditions. For half a baby is not half of a living and growing child.

It is a waste of time to worry about what will be acceptable and what the decision maker should or should not say so as not to evoke resistance. (The things one worries about seldom happen, while objections and difficulties no one thought about may suddenly turn out to be almost insurmountable obstacles.) In other words, the decision maker gains nothing by starting out with the question, "What is acceptable?" For in the process of answering it, he or she usually gives away the important things and loses any chance to come up with an effective–let alone the right–answer.

The Action

Converting the decision into action is the fifth major element in the decision process. While thinking through the boundary conditions is the most difficult step in decision making, converting the decision into effective action is usually the most time-consuming one. Yet a decision will not become effective unless the action commitments have been built into it from the start. In fact, no decision has been made unless carrying it out in specific steps has become someone's work assignment and responsibility. Until then, it is only a good intention.

The flaw in so many policy statements, especially those of business, is that they contain no action commitment—to carry them out is no one's specific work and responsibility. Small wonder then that the people in the organization tend to view such statements cynically, if not as declarations of what top management is really *not* going to do.

Converting a decision into action requires answering several distinct questions: Who has to know of this decision? What action has to be taken? Who is to take it? What does the action have to be so that the people who have to do it *can* do it? The first and the last of these questions are too often overlooked—with dire results. A story that has become a legend among operations researchers illustrates the importance of the question, "Who has to know?":

> A major manufacturer of industrial equipment decided several years ago to discontinue one of its models that had for years been standard equipment on a line of machine tools, many of which were still in use. It was, therefore, decided to sell the model to present owners of the old equipment for another three years as a replacement, and then to stop making and selling it. Orders for this particular model had been going down for a good many years. But they shot up immediately as customers reordered against the day when the model would no longer be available. No one had, however, asked, "Who needs to know of this decision?"
>
> Consequently, nobody informed the purchasing clerk who was in charge of buying the parts from which the model itself was being assembled. His instructions were to buy parts in a given ratio to current sales—and the instructions remained unchanged.

Thus, when the time came to discontinue further production of the model, the company had in its warehouse enough parts for another eight to ten years of production, parts that had to be written off at a considerable loss.

The action must also be appropriate to the capacities of the people who have to carry it out. Thus:

A large U.S. chemical company found itself, in recent years, with fairly large amounts of blocked currency in two West African countries. To protect this money, top management decided to invest it locally in businesses which would: (1) contribute to the local economy, (2) not require imports from abroad, and (3) if successful, be the kind that could be sold to local investors if and when currency remittances became possible again. To establish these businesses, the company developed a simple chemical process to preserve a tropical fruit—a staple crop in both countries—which, up until then, had suffered serious spoilage in transit to its Western markets.

The business was a success in both countries. But in one country the local manager set the business up in such a manner that it required highly skilled and technically trained management of a kind not easily available in West Africa. In the other country, the local manager thought through the capacities of the people who would eventually have to run the business. Consequently, he worked hard at making both the process and the business simple, and at staffing his operation from the start with local nationals right up to the top management level.

A few years later it became possible again to transfer currency from these two countries. But, though the business flourished, no buyer could be found for it in the first country. No one available locally had the necessary managerial and technical skills to run it, and so the business had to be liquidated at a loss. In the other country, so many local entrepreneurs were eager to buy the business that the company repatriated its original investment with a substantial profit.

The chemical process and the business built on it were essentially the same in both places. But in the first country no one had asked, "What kind of people do we have available to make this decision effective? And what can they do?" As a result, the decision itself became frustrated.

This action commitment becomes doubly important when people have to change their behavior, habits, or attitudes if a decision is to become effective. Here, the executive must make sure not only that the responsibility for the action is clearly assigned, but that the people assigned are capable of carrying it out. Thus the decision maker has to make sure that the measurements, the standards for accomplishment, and the incentives of those charged with the action responsibility are changed simultaneously. Otherwise, the organization people will get caught in a paralyzing internal emotional conflict. Consider these two examples:

- When Theodore Vail was president of the Bell Telephone System 60 years ago, he decided that its business was service. This decision explains in large part why the United States (and Canada) has today an investor-owned, rather than a nationalized, telephone system. Yet this policy statement might have remained a dead letter if Vail had not at the same time designed yardsticks of service performance and introduced these as a means to measure, and ultimately to reward, managerial performance. The Bell managers of that time were used to being measured by the profitability (or at least by the cost) of their units. The new yardsticks resulted in the rapid acceptance of the new objectives.

- In sharp contrast is the recent failure of a brilliant chairman and chief executive to make effective a new organization structure and new objectives in an old, large, and proud U.S. company. Everyone agreed that the changes were needed. The company, after many years as leader of its industry, showed definite signs of aging. In many markets newer, smaller, and more aggressive competitors were outflanking it. But contrary to the action required to gain acceptance for the new ideas, the chairman–in order to placate the opposition–promoted prominent spokesmen of the old school into the most visible and highest salaried positions–in particular into three new executive vice presidencies. This meant only one thing to the people in the company: "They don't really mean it." If the greatest rewards are given for behavior contrary to that which the new course of action requires, then everyone will conclude that this is what the people at the top really want and are going to reward.

Only the most effective executive can do what Vail did–build the execution of his decision into the decision itself. But every executive can think through what action commitments a specific decision requires, what work assignments follow from it, and what people are available to carry it out.

The Feedback

Finally, information monitoring and reporting have to be built into the decision to provide continuous testing, against actual events, of the expectations that underlie the decisions. Decisions are made by people. People are fallible; at best, their works do not last long. Even the best decision has a high probability of being wrong. Even the most effective one eventually becomes obsolete.

This surely needs no documentation. And every executive always builds organized feedback–reports, figures, studies–into his or her decision to monitor and report on it. Yet far too many decisions fail to achieve their anticipated results, or indeed ever to become effective, despite all these feedback reports. Just as the view from the Matterhorn cannot be visualized by studying a map of Switzerland (one abstraction), a decision cannot be fully and accurately evaluated by studying a report. That is because reports are, of necessity, abstractions.

Effective decision makers know this and follow a rule which the military developed long ago. The commander who makes a decision does not depend on reports to see how it is being carried out. The commander or an aide goes and looks. The reason is not that effective decision makers (or effective commanders) distrust their subordinates. Rather, they learned the hard way to distrust abstract "communications."

With the coming of the computer this feedback element will become even more important, for the decision maker will in all likelihood be even further removed from the scene of action. Unless he or she accepts, as a matter of course, that he or she had better go out and look at the scene of action, he or she will be increasingly divorced from reality. All a computer can handle is abstractions. And abstractions can be relied on only if they are constantly checked against concrete results. Otherwise, they are certain to mislead.

To go and look is also the best, if not the only way, for an executive to test whether the assumptions on which the decision has been made are still valid or whether they are becoming obsolete and need to be thought through again. And the executive always has to expect the assumptions to become obsolete sooner or later. Reality never stands still very long.

Failure to go out and look is the typical reason for persisting in a course of action long after it has ceased to be appropriate or even rational. This is true for business decisions as well as for governmental policies. It explains in large measure the failure of Stalin's cold war policy in Europe, but also the inability of the United States to adjust its policies to the realities of a Europe restored to prosperity and economic growth, and the failure of the British to accept, until too late, the reality of the European Common Market. Moreover, in any business I know, failure to go out and look at customers and markets, at competitors and their products, is also a major reason for poor, ineffectual, and wrong decisions.

Decision makers need organized information for feedback. They need reports and figures. But unless they build their feedback around direct exposure to reality–unless they discipline themselves to go out and look–they condemn themselves to a sterile dogmatism.

Concluding Note

Decision making is only one of the tasks of an executive. It usually takes but a small fraction of his or her time. But to make the important decisions is the *specific* executive task. Only an executive makes such decisions.

An *effective* executive makes these decisions as a systematic process with clearly defined elements and in a distinct sequence of steps. Indeed, to be expected (by virtue of position or knowledge) to make decisions that have significant and positive impact on the entire organization, its performance, and its results characterizes the effective executive.

3 How to Make
People Decisions

EXECUTIVES spend more time on managing people and making people decisions than on anything else–and they should. No other decisions are so long lasting in their consequences or so difficult to unmake. And yet, by and large, executives make poor promotion and staffing decisions. By all accounts, their batting average is no better than 0.333: at most one-third of such decisions turn out right; one-third are minimally effective; and one-third are outright failures.

In no other area of management would we put up with such miserable performance. Indeed, we need not and should not. Managers making people decisions will never be perfect, of course, but they should come pretty close to batting 1,000–especially since in no other area of management do we know as much.

Some executives' people decisions have, however, approached perfection. At the time of Pearl Harbor, every single general officer in the U.S. Army was overage. Although none of the younger men had been tested in combat or in a significant troop command, the United States came out of World War II with the largest corps of competent general officers any army has ever had. George C. Marshall, the army's chief of staff, had personally chosen each man. Not all were great successes, but practically none were outright failures.

In the 40 or so years during which he ran General Motors, Alfred P. Sloan, Jr. picked every GM executive–down to the manufacturing

July–August 1985

managers, controllers, engineering managers, and master mechanics at even the smallest accessory division. By today's standards, Sloan's vision and values may seem narrow. They were. He was concerned only with performance in and for GM. Nonetheless, his long-term performance in placing people in the right jobs was flawless.

The Basic Principles

There is no such thing as an infallible judge of people, at least not on this side of the Pearly Gates. There are, however, a few executives who take their people decisions seriously and work at them.

Marshall and Sloan were about as different as two human beings can be, but they followed, and quite consciously, much the same principles in making people decisions:

- If I put a person into a job and he or she does not perform, I have made a mistake. I have no business blaming that person, no business invoking the "Peter Principle," no business complaining. I have made a mistake.

- "The soldier has a right to competent command" was already an old maxim at the time of Julius Caesar. It is the duty of managers to make sure that the responsible people in their organizations perform.

- Of all the decisions an executive makes, none are as important as the decisions about people because they determine the performance capacity of the organization. Therefore, I'd better make these decisions well.

- The one "don't": do not give new people new major assignments, for doing so only compounds the risks. Give this sort of assignment to someone whose behavior and habits you know and who has earned trust and credibility within your organization. Put a high-level newcomer first into an established position where the expectations are known and help is available.

Some of the worst staffing failures I have seen involved brilliant Europeans hired by U.S. companies—one based in Pittsburgh; the other, Chicago—to head up new European ventures. Dr. Hans Schmidt and M. Jean Perrin (only the names are fictitious) were hailed as geniuses when they came in. A year later they were both out, totally defeated.

No one in Pittsburgh had understood that Schmidt's training and temperament would make him sit on a new assignment for the first six or nine months, thinking, studying, planning, getting ready for decisive action. Schmidt, in turn, had never even imagined that Pittsburgh expected instant action and immediate results. No one in Chicago had known that Perrin, while a solid and doggedly purposeful man, was excitable and mercurial, flailing his arms, making speeches about trivia, and sending up one trial balloon after another. Although both men subsequently became highly successful CEOs of major European corporations, both executives were failures in companies that did not know and understand them.

Two other U.S. companies successfully established businesses for the first time in Europe during the same period (the late 1960s and early 1970s). To initiate their projects, each sent to Europe a U.S. executive who had never before worked or lived there but whom people in the head offices knew thoroughly and understood well. In turn the two managers were thoroughly familiar with their companies. At the same time, each organization hired half a dozen young Europeans and placed them in upper-middle executive jobs in the United States. Within a few years, both companies had a solid European business and a trained, seasoned, and trusted corps of executives to run it.

As Winston Churchill's ancestor, the great Duke of Marlborough, observed some three centuries ago, "The basic trouble in coalition warfare is that one has to entrust victory if not one's life, to a fellow commander whom one knows by reputation rather than by performance."

In the corporation as in the military, without personal knowledge built up over a period of time there can be neither trust nor effective communication.

The Decision Steps

Just as there are only a few basic principles, there are only a few important steps to follow in making effective promotion and staffing decisions:

Think through the assignment

Job descriptions may last a long time. In one large manufacturing company, for example, the job description for the position of division general manager has hardly changed since the company began to decentralize 30 years ago. Indeed, the job description for bishops in the Roman Catholic church has not changed at all since canon law was first codified in the thirteenth century. But assignments change all the time, and unpredictably.

Once in the early 1940s, I told Alfred Sloan that he seemed to spend an inordinate amount of time pondering the assignment of a fairly low-level job—general sales manager of a small accessory division—before choosing among three equally qualified candidates. "Look at the assignment the last few times we had to fill the same job," Sloan answered. To my surprise, I found that the terms of the assignment were quite different on each occasion.

When putting a man in as division commander during World War II, George Marshall always looked first at the nature of the assignment for the next eighteen months or two years. To raise a division and train it is one assignment. To lead it in combat is quite another. To take command of a division that has been badly mauled and restore its morale and fighting strength is another still.

When the task is to select a new regional sales manager, the responsible executive must first know what the heart of the assignment is: to recruit and train new salespeople because, say, the present sales force is nearing retirement age? Or is it to open up new markets because the company's products, though doing well with old-line industries in the region, have not been able to penetrate new and growing markets? Or, since the bulk of sales still comes from products that are 25 years old, is it to establish a market presence for the company's new products? Each of these is a different assignment and requires a different kind of person.

Look at a number of potentially qualified people

The controlling word here is "number." Formal qualifications are a minimum for consideration; their absence disqualifies the candidate automatically. Equally important, the person and the assignment need to fit each other. To make an effective decision, an executive should look at three to five qualified candidates.

Think hard about how to look at these candidates

If an executive has studied the assignment, he or she understands what a new person would need to do with high priority and concentrated effort. The central question is not "What can this or that candidate do or not do?" It is, rather, "What are the strengths each possesses and are these the right strengths for the assignment?" Weaknesses are limitations, which may, of course, rule a candidate out. For instance, a person may be excellently qualified for the technical aspects of a job; but if the assignment requires above all the ability to build a team and this ability is lacking, then the fit is not right.

But effective executives do not start out by looking at weaknesses. You cannot build performance on weaknesses. You can build only on strengths. Both Marshall and Sloan were highly demanding men, but both knew that what matters is the ability to do the assignment. If that exists, the company can always supply the rest. If it does not exist, the rest is useless.

If, for instance, a division needed an officer for a training assignment, Marshall looked for people who could turn recruits into soldiers. Every man that was good at this task usually had serious weaknesses in other areas. One was not particularly effective as a tactical commander and was positively hopeless when it came to strategy. Another had foot-in-mouth disease and got into trouble with the press. A third was vain, arrogant, egotistical, and fought constantly with his commanding officer. Never mind, could he train recruits? If the answer was yes—and especially if the answer was "he's the best"—he got the job.

In picking the members of their cabinets, Franklin Roosevelt and Harry Truman said, in effect: "Never mind personal weaknesses. Tell me first what each of them can do." It may not be coincidence that these two presidents had the strongest cabinets in twentieth-century U.S. history.

Discuss each of the candidates with several people who have worked with them

One executive's judgment alone is worthless. Because all of us have first impressions, prejudices, likes, and dislikes, we need to listen to what other people think. When the military picks general officers or the Catholic church picks bishops, this kind of extensive discussion is a formal step in their selection process. Competent executives do it informally. Hermann Abs, the former head of Deutsche Bank, picked more successful chief executives in recent times than anyone else. He personally chose most of the top-level managers who pulled off the postwar German "economic miracle," and he checked out each of them first with three or four of the person's former bosses or colleagues.

Make sure the appointee understands the job

After the appointee has been in a new job for three or four months, he or she should be focusing on the demands of that job rather than on the requirements of preceding assignments. It is the executive's responsibility to call that person in and say, "You have now been regional sales manager–or whatever–for three months. What do you have to do to be a success in your new job? Think it through and come back in a week or ten days and show me in writing. But I can tell you one thing right away: the things you did to get the promotion are almost certainly the wrong things to do now."

If you do not follow this step, don't blame the candidate for poor performance. Blame yourself. You have failed in your duty as a manager.

The largest single source of failed promotions–and I know of no greater waste in U.S. management–is the failure to think through, and help others think through, what a new job requires. All too typical is the brilliant former student of mine who telephoned me a few months ago, almost in tears. "I got my first big chance a year ago," he said. "My company made me engineering manager. Now they tell me that I'm through. And yet I've done a better job than ever before. I have actually designed three successful new products for which we'll get patents."

It is only human to say to ourselves, "I must have done something right or I would not have gotten the big new job. Therefore, I had better do more of what I did to get the promotion now that I have it." It is not intuitively obvious to most people that a new and different job requires new and different behavior. Almost 50 years ago, a boss of mine challenged me four months after he had advanced me to a far more responsible position. Until he called me in, I had continued to do what I had done before. To his credit, he understood that it was his responsibility to make me see that a new job means different behavior, a different focus, and different relationships.

The High-Risk Decisions

Even if executives follow all these steps, some of their people decisions will still fail. These are, for the most part, the high-risk decisions that nevertheless have to be taken.

There is, for example, high risk in picking managers in professional organizations—for a research lab, say, or an engineering or corporate legal department. Professionals do not readily accept as their boss someone whose credentials in the field they do not respect. In choosing a manager of engineering, the choices are therefore limited to the top-flight engineers in the department. Yet there is no correlation (unless it be a negative one) between performance as a bench engineer and performance as a manager. Much the same is true when a high-performing operating manager gets a promotion to a staff job in headquarters or a staff expert moves into a line position. Temperamentally, operating people are frequently un-suited to the tensions, frustrations, and relationships of staff work, and vice versa. The first-rate regional sales manager may well become totally ineffective if promoted into market research, sales fore-casting, or pricing.

We do not know how to test or predict whether a person's tempera-ment will suit a new environment. We can find this out only by experience. If a move from one kind of work to another does not pan out, the executive who made the decision has to remove the misfit, and fast. But that executive also has to say, "I made a mistake, and it is my job to correct it." To keep misfits in a job they cannot do is not being kind; it is being cruel. But there is also no reason to let the person go. A company can always use a good bench engineer, a good analyst, a good sales manager. The proper course of action—and it works most times—is to offer the misfit a return to the old job or an equivalent.

People decisions may also fail because a job has become what New England ship captains 150 years ago called a "widow maker." When a clipper ship, no matter how well designed and constructed, began to have fatal "accidents," the owners did not redesign or rebuild the ship. They broke it up as fast as possible.

Widow makers—that is, jobs that regularly defeat even good people—appear most often when a company grows or changes fast. For instance, in the 1960s and early 1970s, the job of "international vice president" in U.S. banks became a widow maker. It had always been an easy job to fill. In fact, it had long been considered a job in which banks could safely put "also rans" and could expect them to perform well. Then, suddenly, the job began to defeat one new incumbent after another. What had happened, as hindsight now tells us, is that international activity quickly and without warning became an integral part of the daily business of major banks and their corporate customers. What had been until then an easy job became, literally, a "nonjob" that nobody could do.

Whenever a job defeats two people in a row, who in their earlier assignments had performed well, a company has a widow maker on its hands. When this happens, a responsible executive should not ask the headhunter for a universal genius. Instead abolish the job. Any job that ordinarily competent people cannot perform is a job that cannot be staffed. Unless changed, it will predictably defeat the third incumbent the way it defeated the first two.

Making the right people decisions is the ultimate means of controlling an organization well. Such decisions reveal how competent management is, what its values are, and whether it takes its job seriously. No matter how hard managers try to keep their decisions a secret—and some still try hard—people decisions cannot be hidden. They are eminently visible.

Executives often cannot judge whether a strategic move is a wise one. Nor are they necessarily interested. "I don't know why we are buying this business in Australia, but it won't interfere with what we are doing here in Fort Worth" is a common reaction. But when the same executives read that "Joe Smith has been made controller in the XYZ division," they usually know Joe much better than top management does. These executives should be able to say, "Joe deserves the promotion; he is an excellent choice–just the person that division needs to get the controls appropriate for its rapid growth."

If, however, Joe got promoted because he is a politician, everybody will know it. They will all say to themselves, "Okay, that is the way to get ahead in this company." They will despise their management for forcing them to become politicians but will either quit or become politicians themselves in the end. As we have known for a long time, people in organizations tend to behave as they see others being rewarded. And when the rewards go to nonperformance, to flattery, or to mere cleverness, the organization will soon decline into non-performance, flattery, or cleverness.

Executives who do not make the effort to get their people decisions right do more than risk poor performance. They risk losing their organization's respect.

4 The Big Power
of Little Ideas

- Is long-range planning for the big company only?

- Does LRP mean predicting what the future will hold and adapting company actions to the anticipated trends?

Many executives, judging by their actions, would answer *yes* to both these questions. But they are wrong. The correct answer to both is a resounding *no!*

The future cannot be known. The only thing certain about it is that it will be different from, rather than a continuation of, today. But the future is as yet unborn, unformed, undetermined. It can be shaped by purposeful action. And the one thing that can effectively motivate such action is an idea—an idea of a different economy, a different technology, or a different market exploited by a different business.

But ideas always start small. That is why long-range planning is not just for the large company. That is why the small business may actually have an advantage in attempting to shape the future today.

The new, the different, when judged in dollars, always looks so small and insignificant that it tends to be dwarfed by the sheer volume of the existing business in the large company. The few million dollars in sales which a new idea might produce in the next few years, even if wildly successful, look so puny compared to the

May–June 1964

hundreds of millions the existing businesses of the large company produce that these dollars are sometimes disregarded.

And yet the new requires a great deal of effort. So much so that the small company is often far more willing to tackle the job. This is why there is good reason for the large company to organize special long-range planning effort; otherwise it may never get around to anything but today's work.

But, of course, the small company that does a good job of shaping the future today will not remain a "small business" very long. Every successful large business in existence was once—and often quite recently, as in the case of IBM or Xerox—a small business based on an idea of what the future should be.

This "idea," however, has to be an entrepreneurial one—with potential and capacity for producing wealth—expressed in a going, working, producing business, and effective through business actions and business behavior. Underlying the entrepreneurial idea is always the question: "What major change in economy, market, or knowledge would enable our company to conduct business the way we really would *like* to do it, the way we would really obtain the best economic results?" The dominant question should not be: "What should future society look like?" This is the question of the social reformer, the revolutionary, or the philosopher—not the entrepreneur.

Because this seems so limited, so self-centered an approach, historians have tended to overlook it. They have tended to be oblivious of the impact of the innovating businessman. The *great* philosophical idea has had, of course, much more profound effects. But, on the other hand, very few philosophical ideas have had any effect at all. And while each business idea is much more limited, larger proportions of them are effective. As a result, innovating businessmen as a group have had a good deal more impact on society than historians realize.

The very fact that theirs are not "big ideas"—ones which encompass all of society or all of knowledge, but "little ideas" which affect just one narrow area—makes the ideas of the entrepreneur much more viable. The people who possess such ideas may be wrong about everything else in the future economy or society. But what does it matter so long as they are approximately right in respect to their own, narrow business focus? All that they need to be successful is just *one* small, specific development. It is true that a few–a very few–big philosophical ideas do become footnotes in history books; however, a great many small entrepreneurial ideas become stock market listings.

Let us turn to history for some little ideas that have led to large results. First, let us note some ideas from which whole industries grew. (Afterward we will look at some ideas from which great corporations have sprung.)

Commercial Banking

The entrepreneurial innovation that has had the greatest impact was that which converted the theoretical proposition of the French social philosopher, Claude Henri Saint-Simon, into a bank a century ago. Saint-Simon had started with the concept of the entrepreneur as developed earlier by his compatriot, the economist J. B. Say, to develop a philosophical system around the creative role of capital.

Saint-Simon's idea became effective through a banking business: the famous Crédit Mobilier which his disciples, the brothers Pereire, founded in Paris during the middle of the nineteenth century. The Crédit Mobilier was to be the conscious developer of industry through the direction of the liquid resources of the community. It came to be the prototype for the entire banking system of the then "underdeveloped" continent of Europe of the Pereires' days– beginning with France, the Netherlands, and Belgium. The Pereires' imitators then founded the business banks of Germany, Switzerland, Austria, Scandinavia, and Italy, which became the main agents for the industrial development of these countries.

After our Civil War the idea crossed the Atlantic. The U.S. bankers who developed U.S. industry–from Jay Cooke and the American Crédit Mobilier, which financed the transcontinental railroad, to J. P. Morgan–were all imitators of the Pereires, whether they knew it or not. So were the Japanese *zaibatsu*–the great banker-industrialists who built the foundations for the economy of modern Japan.

The most faithful disciple of the Pereires, however, has been Soviet Russia. The idea of planning through controlled allocation of capital has been taken directly from the Pereires. There is nothing of this in Marx, above all no planning. All the Soviets actually did was to substitute the state for the individual banker. This was actually a step taken by an Austrian, Rudolf Hilferding, who started out in Vienna as a banker in the business bank tradition and ended as the leading theoretician of German democratic socialism. Hilferding's book, *Finance Capital* (1910), was acknowledged by Lenin to have been the source of his planning and industrialization concepts.

Every single "development bank" started today in an underdeveloped country is still a direct descendant of the original Crédit Mobilier. But the point about the Crédit Mobilier is not that it has had tremendous worldwide impact. The point is that the Pereires started a business—a bank with the intention of making money.

Chemical Industry

By all odds, the modern chemical industry should have arisen in England. In the mid-nineteenth century, England, with its highly developed textile industry, was the major market for chemicals. It also was the home of the scientific leaders of the time—Michael Faraday and Charles Darwin.

The modern chemical industry did actually start with an English discovery: Perkin's discovery of aniline dyes in 1856. Yet 20 years after Perkin's discovery (around 1875) leadership in the new industry had clearly passed to Germany. German businessmen contributed the entrepreneurial idea that was lacking in England: the result of scientific inquiry, organic chemistry in this case, can be directly converted into marketable applications.

Modern Merchandising

The most powerful private business in history was probably managed by the Japanese House of Mitsui, which before its dissolution after World War II was estimated by American occupation authorities to have employed one million people throughout the world. Its origin was the world's first department store, developed in Tokyo during the mid-seventeenth century by an early Mitsui.

The entrepreneurial idea underlying this business was that of the merchant as a principal of economic life, not as a mere middleman. This meant fixed prices to the customer. And it also meant that the Mitsuis no longer acted as agents in dealing with craftsmen and manufacturers. They would buy for their own account and give orders for standardized merchandise to be made according to their specifications. In overseas trade the merchant had acted as a principal all along. However, by 1650 overseas trade had been suppressed in Japan, and the Mitsuis promptly took the overseas-trade concepts and built a domestic merchant-business on them.

Mass Distribution

Great imagination is not necessary to make an entrepreneurial idea successful. All that may be needed is systematic work which will make effective in the future something that has already occurred. Typically, for instance, new developments in the economy and market will run well ahead of distribution. Organizing the distribution, however, may make the change effective—and thereby create a true growth business.

A Canadian, Willard Garfield Weston, saw, for instance, that while the English housewives had come, by the end of World War II, to demand packaged, sliced bread, there was no adequate distribution system to supply them with what they wanted to buy where they wanted to buy it. Because of this small idea one of the largest food-marketing companies in Great Britain was established in a few years.

Today similar distribution opportunities may exist in this country as a result of our massive shift to being a society and economy of "knowledge workers"—that is, people with a high degree of formal education who apply knowledge to work, rather than manual skill or brawn. Education itself is perhaps our biggest and fastest growing market—not only schools and colleges, but also industry with its myriads of training programs, the government, and the armed services.

The office supply market—which delivers whatever the knowledge worker needs to be productive, from paper clips to office reproduction equipment and giant computers—is therefore a major growth market. But while this industry and education are each becoming a true mass market, neither has mass distribution yet. The business that organizes distribution in either market today may well be the Sears, Roebuck of tomorrow.

Discount Chains

The rise of the discount house began in the late 1940s with the application of an idea developed by Sears, Roebuck and Co. almost 20 years earlier. Sears, Roebuck became our leading appliance seller in the 1930s when it began to use a sample of each appliance on the store floor solely to demonstrate the merchandise. The appliance purchased by the customer was delivered straight from the warehouse—which realized savings in costs of uncrating, recrating, and shipping of up to 20 percent of retail price. Sears, Roebuck made no secret of this; yet there were few imitators of this idea. After World War II there was one small Chicago appliance merchant who adapted the idea to other makers' products. Today Saul Polk is credited with creating the first and largest and one of the most profitable discount chains in existence.

Little ideas have frequently been the seeds from which giant corporations have grown. Here are a few instances.

IBM

Thomas J. Watson, Sr., who founded and built IBM, did not see the coming development of business technology. But he had the idea of data processing as a unifying concept on which to build a business. IBM was, for a long time, fairly small and confined itself to such mundane work as keeping accounting ledgers and time records. But it was ready to jump when the technology came in—from totally unrelated wartime work—which made data processing by electronic computers actually possible.

While Watson built a small and unspectacular business during the 1920s by designing, selling, and installing punch-card equipment, the logical positivists (e.g., Perry Bridgman in the United States, Rudolph Carnap in Austria) talked and wrote on the systematic methodology of "quantification" and "universal measurements." It is most unlikely that they ever heard of the young struggling IBM company, and certain that they did not connect their ideas with it. Yet it was Watson's IBM and not their philosophical ideas which became operational when the new technology emerged during World War II.

Sears, Roebuck

The men who built Sears, Roebuck and Co.–Richard Sears, Julius Rosenwald, and Albert Loeb, and finally General Robert E. Wood–had active social concerns and lively social imaginations. But not one of them thought of remaking the economy. I doubt that even the idea of a *mass market*–as opposed to the traditional *class market*–occurred to them until long after 1930. From its early beginning, the founders of Sears, Roebuck had the idea that the poor man's money could be made to have the same purchasing power as the rich man's.

But this was not a particularly new idea. Social reformers and economists had bandied it around for decades. The cooperative movement in Europe grew mainly out of it. Sears, Roebuck was, however, the first business in the United States built on this idea. It started with the question: "What would make the farmer a customer for a retail business?" The answer was simple: "He needs to be sure of getting goods of the same dependable quality as do city people but at a low price." In 1900 or even 1920 this was an idea of considerable audacity.

Bata

The basic entrepreneurial idea may be merely an imitation of something that works well in another country or in another industry. For example, when Tomas Bata, the Slovakian shoemaker, returned to Europe from the United States after World War I, he had the idea that everybody in Czechoslovakia and the Balkans could have shoes to wear as did everybody in the United States. "The peasant goes barefoot," he is reported to have said, "not because he is too poor, but because there are no shoes." What was needed to make this vision of a shod peasant come true was someone supplying him with cheap, standardized, but well-designed and durable footwear as was done in the United States.

On the basis of this analogy with America, Bata began without capital in a rented shack and in a few years built pre-Nazi Europe's largest shoe business and one of Europe's most successful companies. Yet to apply U.S. mass-production methods to European consumer goods was hardly a very original idea in the 1920s when Henry Ford and his assembly line were all the rage in Europe. The only original thing was willingness to act on the idea.

To make the future happen requires work rather than "genius." The man with a creative imagination will have more imaginative ideas, to be sure. But whether the more imaginative ideas will actually turn out to be more successful is by no means certain.

Creativity, which looms so large in present discussions of innovation, is not the real problem. There are usually more ideas in any organization, including businesses, than can possibly be put to use.[1] Ask any company—including seemingly moribund ones—this question: "What in our economy, or our society, or our state of knowledge would give our business its greatest opportunity if only we could make it happen?" Dozens of responses will burst from management's lips. As a rule we are not lacking *ideas*—not even good, serviceable ideas. What is lacking is management's *willingness to welcome ideas,* in fact, solicit them, rather than just products or processes. Products and processes, after all, are only the vehicles through which the ideas become effective. The specific future products and processes often cannot even be imagined.

For example, when Du Pont started the work on polymer chemistry out of which nylon eventually evolved, it did not know that man-made fibers would be the end-product. Du Pont acted on the assumption that any gain in man's ability to manipulate the structure of large, organic molecules—a scientific skill at that time in its infancy—would lead to commercially important results of some kind. It was only after six or seven years of research work that man-made fibers first appeared as a possible major result area.

Indeed, as the IBM experience shows, the specific products and processes that make an idea truly successful often come out of entirely different and unrelated work.

But there must always be a willingness to think in terms of the general rather than the specific, in terms of a business, the contributions it makes, the satisfactions it supplies, the market and economy it serves. This is the entrepreneurial point of view. And it is accessible to the average businessman.

Also, the manager must have the courage to commit resources—and in particular first-rate people—to work on making the future happen. The staffs for this work should be small. But they should contain the very best men available; otherwise, nothing will happen.

The businessman needs a touchstone of validity and practicality for entrepreneurial, future-making ideas. Indeed, the reason some businesses fail to innovate is not that they shy away from ideas. It is that they engage in hopelessly romantic ones—at great cost in men and money. An idea must meet rigorous tests of practicality if it is to be capable of making a business successful in the future.

It must first have operational validity. Can we take action on this idea? Or can we only talk about it? Can we really do something right away to bring about the kind of future we desire? Sears, Roebuck, with its idea of bringing the market to the isolated U.S. farmer, could show immediate results. In contrast, Du Pont with its idea of polymer chemistry could only organize research work on a very small scale. It could only underwrite the research of one first-rate man. But both companies could *do* something right away.

To be able to spend money on research is not enough. It must be research directed toward the realization of the idea. The knowledge sought may be general—as was that of Du Pont's project. But it must be reasonably clear, at least, that, if available, the knowledge gained will be applicable to operations.

The idea must have economic validity. If it could be put to work immediately, it would have to be able to produce economic results. We may not be able to do *all* that we would like to see done—not for a long time, and perhaps never. But if we could do something right away, the resulting products, processes, or services would find a customer, a market, an end use, and would be capable of being sold profitably. In short, they should satisfy a want and need.

Finally, the idea must meet the test of personal commitment. Do we really believe in the idea? Do we really want to be that kind of people, do that kind of work, run that kind of business?

To make the future demands courage. It demands work. But it also demands faith. To commit oneself to the expedient is simply not practical. It will not suffice for the trials ahead. For no such idea is foolproof—nor should it be.

The one idea about the future that *must* fail is the apparently sure thing, the riskless idea, which is believed to be incapable of failure. The ideas on which tomorrow's business is to be built *must* be uncertain; no one can really say, as yet, what they will look like if and when they become reality. They *must* be risky; they have a probability of success, of course, but also a probability of failure. If they are not both uncertain and risky, they are simply not practical ideas for the future.

Conclusion

It is not absolutely necessary for every business to search for the idea that will make the future, and to start work on its realization. Indeed, a good many managements do not even make their present business effective—and yet their company somehow survives for a while. Big businesses, in particular, seem able to coast a long time on the courage, work, and vision of earlier executives before they erode and run down.

But the future always does come, sooner or later. And it is always different. Even the mightiest company will be in trouble if it does not work toward the future. It will lose distinction and leadership. All that will be left is big-company overhead. It will neither control not understand what is happening.

By not daring to take the risk of making the new happen, management takes, by default, the greater risk of being surprised by what will happen. This is a risk that even the largest and richest company cannot afford to take. And it is a risk that not even the smallest company need take.

5   The Discipline
of Innovation

DESPITE much discussion these days of the "entrepreneurial personality," few of the entrepreneurs with whom I have worked during the last 30 years had such personalities. But I have known many people–salespeople, surgeons, journalists, scholars, even musicians–who did have them without being the least bit "entrepreneurial." What all the successful entrepreneurs I have met have in common is not a certain kind of personality but a commitment to the systematic practice of innovation.

Innovation is the specific function of entrepreneurship, whether in an existing business, a public service institution, or a new venture started by a lone individual in the family kitchen. It is the means by which the entrepreneur either creates new wealth-producing resources or endows existing resources with enhanced potential for creating wealth.

Today, much confusion exists about the proper definition of entrepreneurship. Some observers use the term to refer to all small businesses; others, to all new businesses. In practice, however, a great many well-established businesses engage in highly successful entrepreneurship. The term, then, refers not to an enterprise's size or age, but to a certain kind of activity. At the heart of that activity is innovation: the effort to create purposeful, focused change in an enterprise's economic or social potential.

May–June 1985

Sources of Innovation

There are, of course, innovations that spring from a flash of genius. Most innovations, however, especially the successful ones, result from a conscious, purposeful search for innovation opportunities, which are found only in a few situations.

Four such areas of opportunity exist *within* a company or industry:

Unexpected occurrences.
Incongruities.
Process needs.
Industry and market changes.

Three additional sources of opportunity exist *outside* a company in its social and intellectual environment:

Demographic changes.
Changes in perception.
New knowledge.

True, these sources overlap, different as they may be in the nature of their risk, difficulty, and complexity, and the potential for innovation may well lie in more than one area at a time. But among them, they account for the great majority of all innovation opportunities.

Unexpected Occurrences

Consider, first, the easiest and simplest source of innovation opportunity: the unexpected. In the early 1930s, IBM developed the first modern accounting machine, which was designed for banks, but banks in 1933 did not buy new equipment. What saved the company— according to a story that Thomas Watson, Sr., the company's founder and long-term CEO, often told—was its exploitation of an unexpected success: the New York Public Library wanted to buy a machine. Unlike the banks, libraries in those early New Deal days had money, and Watson sold more than a hundred of his otherwise unsalable machines to libraries.

Fifteen years later, when everyone believed that computers were designed for advanced scientific work, business unexpectedly showed an interest in a machine that could do payroll. Univac, which had the most advanced machine, spurned business applications. But

IBM immediately realized it faced a possible unexpected success, redesigned what was basically Univac's machine for such mundane applications as payroll, and within five years became the leader in the computer industry, a position it has maintained to this day.

The unexpected failure may be an equally important innovation opportunity source. Everyone knows about the Ford Motor Company's Edsel as the biggest new car failure in automotive history. What very few people seem to know, however, is that the Edsel's failure was the foundation for much of the company's later success. Ford planned the Edsel, the most carefully designed car to that point in American automotive history, to give the company a full product line with which to compete with GM. When it bombed, despite all the planning, market research, and design that had gone into it, Ford realized that something was happening in the automobile market that ran counter to the basic assumptions on which GM and everyone else had been designing and marketing cars. No longer did the market segment primarily by income groups; suddenly, the new principle of segmentation was what we now call "life-styles." Ford's immediate responses were the Mustang and the Thunderbird—the cars that gave the company a distinct personality and reestablished it as an industry leader.

Unexpected successes and failures are such productive sources of innovation opportunities because most businesses dismiss them, disregard them, and even resent them. The German scientist who around 1906 synthesized novocaine, the first nonaddictive narcotic, had intended it to be used in major surgical procedures like amputation. Surgeons, however, preferred total anesthesia for such procedures; they still do. Instead, novocaine found a ready appeal among dentists. Its inventor spent the remaining years of his life traveling from dental school to dental school making speeches that forbade dentists to "misuse" his noble invention in applications for which he had not intended it.

This is a caricature, to be sure, but it illustrates the attitude managers often take to the unexpected: "It should not have happened." Corporate reporting systems further ingrain this reaction, for they draw attention away from unanticipated possibilities. The typical monthly or quarterly report has on its first page a list of problems, that is, the areas where results fall short of expectations. Such information is needed, of course; it helps prevent deterioration of performance.

But it also suppresses the recognition of new opportunities. The first acknowledgment of a possible opportunity usually applies to an area in which a company does better than budgeted. Thus genuinely entrepreneurial businesses have two "first pages"—a problem page and an opportunity page—and managers spend equal time on both.

Incongruities

Alcon Industries was one of the great success stories of the 1960s because Bill Connor, the company's founder, exploited an incongruity in medical technology. The cataract operation is the world's third or fourth most common surgical procedure. During the last 300 years, doctors systematized it to the point that the only "old-fashioned" step left was the cutting of a ligament. Eye surgeons had learned to cut the ligament with complete success, but it was so different a procedure from the rest of the operation and so incompatible with it that they often dreaded it. It was incongruous.

Doctors had known for 50 years about an enzyme that could dissolve the ligament without cutting. All Connor did was to add a preservative to this enzyme that gave it a few months' shelf life. Eye surgeons immediately accepted the new compound, and Alcon found itself with a worldwide monopoly. Fifteen years later, Nestlé bought the company for a fancy price.

Such an incongruity within the logic or rhythm of a process is only one possibility out of which innovation opportunities may arise. Another source is incongruity between economic realities. For instance, whenever an industry has a steadily growing market but falling profit margins—as, say, in the steel industries of developed countries between 1950 and 1970—an incongruity exists. The innovative response: minimills.

An incongruity between expectations and results can also open up possibilities for innovation. For 50 years after the turn of the century, shipbuilders and shipping companies worked hard both to make ships faster and to lower their fuel consumption. Even so, the more successful they were in boosting speed and trimming fuel needs, the worse ocean freighters' economics became. By 1950 or so, the ocean freighter was dying, if not already dead.

All that was wrong, however, was an incongruity between the industry's assumptions and its realities. The real costs did not come from doing work (that is, being at sea) but from not doing work (that is, sitting idle in port). Once managers understood where costs truly lay, the innovations were obvious: the roll-on and roll-off ship and the container ship. These solutions, which involved old technology, simply applied to the ocean freighter what railroads and truckers had been using for 30 years. A shift in viewpoint, not in technology, totally changed the economics of ocean shipping and turned it into one of the major growth industries of the last 20 to 30 years.

Process Needs

Anyone who has ever driven in Japan knows that the country has no modern highway system. Its roads still follow the paths laid down for–or by–oxcarts in the tenth century. What makes the system work for automobiles and trucks is an adaptation of the reflector used on American highways since the early 1930s. This reflector shows each car, which other cars are approaching, from any one of a half-dozen directions. This minor invention, which enables traffic to move smoothly and with a minimum of accidents, exploited a process need.

Around 1909, a statistician at the American Telephone & Telegraph Company (AT&T) projected two curves 15 years out: telephone traffic and American population. Viewed together, they showed that by 1920 or so every single female in the United States would have to work as a switchboard operator. The process need was obvious, and within two years, AT&T had developed and installed the automatic switchboard.

What we now call "media" also had their origin in two process need-based innovations around 1890. One was Mergenthaler's Linotype, which made it possible to produce a newspaper quickly and in large volume; the other was a social innovation, modern advertising, invented by the first true newspaper publishers, Adolph Ochs of the *New York Times,* Joseph Pulitzer of the *New York World,* and William Randolph Hearst. Advertising made it possible for them to distribute news practically free of charge, with the profit coming from marketing.

Industry & Market Changes

Managers may believe that industry structures are ordained by the Good Lord, but they can–and often do–change overnight. Such change creates tremendous opportunity for innovation.

One of American business's great success stories in recent decades is the brokerage firm of Donaldson, Lufkin & Jenrette (DL&J), recently acquired by the Equitable Life Assurance Society. DL&J was founded in 1961 by three young men, all graduates of the Harvard Business School, who realized that the structure of the financial industry was changing as institutional investors became dominant. These young men had practically no capital and no connections. Still, within a few years, their firm had become a leader in the move to negotiated commissions and one of Wall Street's stellar performers. It was the first to be incorporated and go public.

In a similar fashion, changes in industry structure have created massive innovation opportunities for American health care providers. During the last 10 or 15 years, independent surgical and psychiatric clinics, emergency centers, and HMOs have opened throughout the country. Comparable opportunities in telecommunications followed industry upheavals–both in equipment (with the emergence of such companies as ROLM in the manufacturing of private branch exchanges) and in transmission (with the emergence of MCI and Sprint in long-distance service).

When an industry grows quickly–the critical figure seems to be in the neighborhood of a 40 percent growth rate over ten years or less–its structure changes. Established companies, concentrating on defending what they already have, tend not to counterattack when a newcomer challenges them. Indeed, when market or industry structures change, traditional industry leaders again and again neglect the fastest growing market segments. New opportunities rarely fit the way the industry has always approached the market, defined it, or organized to serve it. Innovators therefore have a good chance of being left alone for a long time.

Demographic Changes

Of the outside sources of innovation opportunity, demographics are the most reliable. Demographic events have known lead times; for instance, every person who will be in the American labor force by the year 2000 has already been born. Yet, because policymakers often neglect demographics, those who watch them and exploit them can reap great rewards.

The Japanese are ahead in robotics because they paid attention to demographics. Everyone in the developed countries around 1970 or so knew that there was both a baby bust and an education explosion going on; half or more of the young people were now staying in school beyond high school. Consequently, the number of people available for traditional blue-collar work in manufacturing was bound to decrease and become inadequate by 1990. Everyone knew this, but only the Japanese acted on it and they now have a ten-year lead in robotics.

Much the same is true of Club Mediterranee's success in the travel and resort business. By 1970, thoughtful observers could have seen the emergence of large numbers of affluent and educated young adults in Europe and the United States. Not comfortable with the kind of vacations their working-class parents had enjoyed–the summer weeks at Brighton or Atlantic City–these young people were ideal customers for a new and exotic version of the "hangout" of their teen years.

Managers have known for a long time that demographics matter, but they have always believed that population statistics change slowly. In this century, however, they don't. Indeed, the innovation opportunities that changes in the numbers of people, and their age distribution, education, occupations, and geographic location make possible are among the most rewarding and least risky of entrepreneurial pursuits.

Changes in Perception

"The glass is half-full" and "the glass is half-empty" are descriptions of the same phenomenon but have vastly different meanings. Changing a manager's perception of a glass from half-full to half-empty opens up big innovation opportunities.

All factual evidence indicates, for instance, that in the last 20 years, Americans' health has improved at unprecedented speed–whether measured by mortality rates for the newborn, survival rates for the very old, the incidence of cancers (other than lung cancer), cancer cure rates, or other factors. Even so, collective hypochondria grips the nation. Never before has there been so much concern with health or so much fear about health. Suddenly everything seems to cause cancer or degenerative heart disease or premature loss of memory. The glass is clearly half-empty.

Rather than rejoicing in great improvements in health, Americans seem to be emphasizing how far away they still are from immortality. This view of things has created many opportunities for innovations: markets for new health care magazines, for all kinds of health foods, and for exercise classes and jogging equipment. The fastest growing new U.S. business in 1983 was a company that makes indoor exercise equipment.

A change in perception does not alter facts. It changes their meaning, though—and very quickly. It took less than two years for the computer to change from being perceived as a threat and as something only big businesses would use to something one buys for doing income tax. Economics do not necessarily dictate such a change; in fact, they may be irrelevant. What determines whether people see a glass as half-full or half-empty is mood rather than fact, and change in mood often defies quantification. But it is not exotic or intangible. It is concrete. It can be defined. It can be tested. And it can be exploited for innovation opportunity.

New Knowledge

Among history-making innovations, those based on new knowledge—whether scientific, technical, or social—rank high. They are the superstars of entrepreneurship; they get the publicity and the money. They are what people usually mean when they talk of innovation, though not all innovations based on knowledge are important. Some are trivial.

Knowledge-based innovations differ from all others in the time they take, in their casualty rates, and in their predictability, as well as in the challenges they pose to entrepreneurs. Like most superstars, they can be temperamental, capricious, and hard to direct. They have, for instance, the longest lead time of all innovations. There is a protracted span between the emergence of new knowledge and its distillation into usable technology. Then, there is another long period before this new technology appears in the marketplace in products, processes, or services. Overall, the lead time involved is something like 50 years, a figure that has not shortened appreciably throughout history.

To become effective, innovation of this sort usually demands not one kind of knowledge but many. Consider one of the most potent knowledge-based innovations: modern banking. The theory of the entrepreneurial bank–that is, of the purposeful use of capital to generate economic development–was formulated by Claude Henri, Comte de Saint-Simon, during the era of Napoleon. Despite Saint-Simon's extraordinary prominence, it was not until 30 years after his death in 1826 that two of his disciples, the brothers Jacob and Isaac Pereire, established the first entrepreneurial bank, the Crédit Mobilier, and ushered in what we now call "finance capitalism."

The Pereires, however, did not know modern commercial banking, which developed at about the same time across the channel in England. The Crédit Mobilier failed ignominiously. Ten years later, two young men–one an American, J. P. Morgan, and one a German, Georg Siemens–put together the French theory of entrepreneurial banking and the English theory of commercial banking to create the first successful modern banks, J. P. Morgan & Company in New York and the Deutsche Bank in Berlin. Another ten years later, a young Japanese, Shibusawa Eiichi, adopted Siemens' concept to his country and thereby laid the foundation of Japan's modern economy. This is how knowledge-based innovation always works.

The computer, to cite another example, required no fewer than six separate strands of knowledge.

Binary arithmetic; Charles Babbage's conception of a calculating machine in the first half of the nineteenth century; the punch card, invented by Herman Hollerith for the U.S. census of 1890; the audion tube, an electronic switch invented in 1906; symbolic logic, which was created between 1910 and 1913 by Bertrand Russell and Alfred North Whitehead; and the concepts of programming and feedback that came out of abortive attempts during World War I to develop effective anti-aircraft guns. Although all the necessary knowledge was available by 1918, the first operational computer did not appear until 1946.

Long lead times and the need for convergence among different kinds of knowledge explain the peculiar rhythm of knowledge-based innovation, its attractions, and its dangers. During a long gestation period, there is a lot of talk and little action. Then, when all the elements suddenly converge, there is tremendous excitement and activity and an enormous amount of speculation. Between 1880 and 1890, for example, almost 1,000 electrical apparatus companies were founded in developed countries. Then, as always, there was a crash and a shakeout. By 1914, only 25 of these companies were still alive. In the early 1920s, 300 to 500 automobile companies existed in the United States; by 1960, only four remained.

It may be difficult, but knowledge-based innovation can be managed. Success requires careful analysis of the various kinds of knowledge needed to make an innovation possible. Both J. P. Morgan and Georg Siemens did this when they established their banking ventures. The Wright brothers did this when they developed the first operational airplane.

Careful analysis of the needs and, above all, the capabilities of the intended user is also essential. It may seem paradoxical, but knowledge-based innovation is more market dependent than any other kind of innovation.

De Havilland, a British company, designed and built the first passenger jet airplane, but it did not analyze what the market needed and therefore did not identify two key factors. One was configuration—that is, the right size with the right payload for the routes on which a jet would give an airline the greatest advantage. The other was equally mundane: how the airlines could finance the purchase of such an expensive plane. Because De Havilland failed to do an adequate user analysis, two American companies, Boeing and Douglas, took over the commercial jet aircraft industry.

Principles of Innovation

Purposeful, systematic innovation begins with the analysis of the sources of new opportunities. Depending on the context, sources will have different importance at different times. Demographics, for instance, may be of little concern to innovators in fundamental industrial processes like steel making, although Mergenthaler's linotype machine became successful primarily because there were not enough skilled typesetters available to satisfy a mass market. By the same token, new knowledge may be of little relevance to someone innovating a social instrument to satisfy a need that changing demographics or tax laws have created. But–whatever the situation–innovators must analyze all opportunity sources.

Because innovation is both conceptual and perceptual, would-be innovators must also go out and look, ask, and listen. Successful innovators use both the right and left sides of their brains. They look at figures. They look at people. They work out analytically what the innovation has to be to satisfy an opportunity. Then they go out and look at potential users to study their expectations, their values, and their needs.

To be effective, an innovation has to be simple and it has to be focused. It should do only one thing; otherwise it confuses people. Indeed, the greatest praise an innovation can receive is for people to say: "This is obvious! Why didn't I think of it? It's so simple!" Even the innovation that creates new users and new markets should be directed toward a specific, clear, and carefully designed application.

Effective innovations start small. They are not grandiose. They try to do one specific thing. It may be to enable a moving vehicle to draw electric power while it runs along rails, the innovation that made possible the electric streetcar. Or it may be the elementary idea of putting the same number of matches into a matchbox (it used to be 50). This simple notion made possible the automatic filling of matchboxes and gave the Swedes a world monopoly on matches for half a century. By contrast, grandiose ideas for things that will "revolutionize an industry" are unlikely to work.

In fact, no one can foretell whether a given innovation will end up a big business or a modest achievement. But even if the results are modest, the successful innovation aims from the beginning to become the standard setter, to determine the direction of a new technology or a new industry, to create the business that is–and remains–ahead of the pack. If an innovation does not aim at leadership from the beginning, it is unlikely to be innovative enough.

Above all, innovation is work rather than genius. It requires knowledge. It often requires ingenuity. And it requires focus. There are clearly people who are more talented as innovators than others but their talents lie in well-defined areas. Indeed, innovators rarely work in more than one area. For all his systematic innovative accomplishments, Edison worked only in the electrical field. An innovator in financial areas, Citibank for example, is not likely to embark on innovations in health care.

In innovation as in any other endeavor, there is talent, there is ingenuity, and there is knowledge. But when all is said and done, what innovation requires is hard, focused, purposeful work. If diligence, persistence, and commitment are lacking, talent, ingenuity, and knowledge are of no avail.

There is, of course, far more to entrepreneurship than systematic innovation: distinct entrepreneurial strategies, for example, and the principles of entrepreneurial management, which are needed equally in the established enterprise, the public service organization, and the new venture. But the very foundation of entrepreneurship—as a practice and as a discipline—is the practice of systematic innovation.

6 Managing for
Business Effectiveness

* *Analysis*   * *Allocation*   * *Decision*

W<small>HAT IS THE</small> first duty—and the continuing responsibility—of the business manager? *To strive for the best possible economic results from the resources currently employed or available.* Everything else managers may be expected to do, or may want to do, rests on sound economic performance and profitable results over the next few years. Even such lofty management tasks as assessing corporate social responsibilities and cultural opportunities are not exempt from this presupposition. And certainly not exempt, by and large, are the individual manager's *own rewards*—money and position.

Accordingly, all business executives spend much, if not all, of their time on the problems of short-run economic performance. They concern themselves with costs and pricing, with scheduling and selling, with quality control and customer service, with purchasing and training. Furthermore, the vast array of tools and techniques available to the modern manager deal to a great extent with managing *today's* business for today's and tomorrow's economic performance. This is the subject matter of 90 out of any 100 books in the business library, and (conservatively) of 90 out of any 100 reports and studies produced within businesses.

May–June 1963

No Time for Clichés

Despite all this attention, few managers I know are greatly impressed with their own performance in this work. They want to know how to organize for the task; how to tell the important from the time-wasting, the potentially effective from the merely frustrating. Despite the flood of data and reports threatening to inundate the manager today, he gets only the vaguest generalities. Such banalities as "low costs" or "high profit margins" are bandied about as answers to the question: What *really* determines economic performance and results in this particular business that I work for?

Even in the boom times of a "seller's market," managing for economic performance tends to be a source of constant frustration. And as soon as times return to normal and markets become competitive again, managing for economic performance tends to generate such confusion, pressure, and anxiety that the decisions made are most unlikely to be the right ones, even for short-run results, let alone for the company's future.[1]

What we need are not more or better tools—we have already many more than any single business (let alone any single manager) can use. What we need are simple concepts—some crude rules of thumb—that will help organize the job by answering:

Just what is the manager's job?
What is the major problem in it?
What is the principle for defining this problem and for analyzing it?

Misplaced Emphasis

I do not propose to give here a full-blown "science of management economics," if only because I have none to give. Even less do I intend to present a magic formula, a "checklist" or "procedure" which will do the job for the manager. For his job is *work*—very hard, demanding, risk-taking work. And while there is plenty of laborsaving machinery around, no one has yet invented a "work-saving" machine, let alone a "think-saving" one.

But I do claim that we know how to organize the job of managing for economic effectiveness and how to do it with both direction and results. The answers to the three key questions above are known, and have been known for such a long time that they should not surprise anyone.

1. *What is the manager's job?* It is to direct the resources and the efforts of the business toward opportunities for economically significant results. This sounds trite–and it is. But every analysis of actual allocation of resources and efforts in business that I have ever seen or made showed clearly that *the bulk of time, work, attention, and money first goes to "problems" rather than to opportunities, and, secondly, to areas where even extraordinarily successful performance will have minimal impact on results.*

2. *What is the major problem?* It is fundamentally the confusion between effectiveness and efficiency that stands between doing the right things and doing things right. *There is surely nothing quite so useless as doing with great efficiency what should not be done at all.* Yet our tools–especially our accounting concepts and data–all focus on efficiency. What we need is (1) a way to identify the areas of effectiveness (of possible significant results), and (2) a method for concentrating on them.

3. *What is the principle?* That, too, is well-known–at least as a general proposition. Business enterprise is not a phenomenon of nature but one of society. In a social situation, however, events are not distributed according to the "normal distribution" of a natural universe (that is, they are not distributed according to the U-shaped Gaussian curve). *In a social situation a very small number of events–10 percent to 20 percent at most–account for 90 percent of all results, whereas the great majority of events account for 10 percent or less of the results.*

This is true in the marketplace. A handful of customers out of many thousands produce the bulk of the orders; a handful of products out of hundreds of items in the line produce the bulk of the volume; and so on. This is true of markets, end uses, and distributive channels. It is equally true of sales efforts: a few salesmen, out of several hundred, always produce two-thirds or more of all new business. It is true in the plant: a handful of production runs account for most of the tonnage. It is true of research: a few men in the laboratory produce all the important innovations, as a rule.

It also holds true for practically all personnel "problems": the great bulk of the grievances always come from a few places or from one group of employees (for example, from the older, unmarried women or from the clean-up men on the night shift), as does the great bulk of absenteeism, of turnover, of suggestions under a suggestion system, and of accidents. As studies at the New York Telephone Company have shown, this is true even in respect to employee sickness.

Revenue Dollars versus Cost Dollars

The importance that this simple statement about "normal distribution" has for managing a business has been grasped by all too few businessmen. It means, first: *while 90 percent of the results are being produced by the first 10 percent of events, 90 percent of the costs are being increased by the remaining and result-less 90 percent of events.*

In other words, costs, too, are a "social phenomenon." If we put it into mathematical language, we see that the "normal distribution curve" of business events is a hyperbola with the results plotted along the plus half, and the costs along the minus half of the curve. Thus, results and costs stand in inverse relationship to each other.

And now, translated back into common language, *economic results are, by and large, directly proportionate to revenue, while costs are directly proportionate to number of transactions.* The only exceptions to this are the purchased materials and parts that go directly into the final product. For example:

- To get a $50,000 order costs no more, as a rule, than to get a $500 order; certainly it does not cost 100 times as much.

- To design a new product that does not sell is as expensive as to design a "winner."

- It costs just as much to do the paper work for a small order as for a large one–the same order entry, production order, scheduling, billing, collecting, and so on.

- It even costs just as much, as a rule, to actually make the product, to package it, and to transport it for a small order as for a large one. Even labor is a "fixed" cost today over any period of time in most manufacturing industries (and in all services) rather than a cost fluctuating with volume. Only purchased materials and parts are truly "variable" costs.

Furthermore, there is the implication that, *"normally," revenues and efforts will allocate themselves to the 90 percent of events that produce practically no results.* They will allocate themselves according to the *number of events* rather than according to results. In fact, the most expensive and potentially most productive resources (i.e., highly trained people) will misallocate themselves the worst. For the pressure exerted by the bulk of transactions is fortified by the person's pride in doing the difficult–whether productive or not.

This has been proved by every single study made; it is, in other words, supported both by principle and by concrete experience. Let me give some examples:

- A large engineering company prided itself on the high quality and reputation of its technical service group, which contained several hundred expensive men. The men were indeed first-rate. But analysis of their allocation showed clearly that they, while working hard, contributed little. Most of them worked on the "interesting" problems–especially those of the very small customers–problems which, even if solved, produced little, if any, business. The automobile industry is the company's major customer and accounts for almost one-third of all purchases. But few technical service people within anyone's memory had even set foot in the engineering department or the plant of an automobile company. "General Motors and Ford don't need us; they have their own people," was their reaction.

- Similarly, in many companies salesmen are misallocated. The largest group of salesmen (and especially the most effective ones) are usually put on the products that are "hard to sell," either because they are "yesterday's products" or because they are "also rans" which managerial vanity desperately is trying to make into "winners." Tomorrow's important products very rarely get the sales effort required. And the product that has sensational success in the market–and which, therefore, ought to be pushed all-out–tends to be slighted. "It is doing all right without extra effort, after all," is the common conclusion.

- Research departments, design staffs, market development efforts, even advertising efforts have been shown to be allocated the same way in lots of companies–by transaction rather than by results, by what is difficult rather than by what is productive, by yesterday's problems rather than by today's and tomorrow's opportunities!

Unaccountable Accounting

"Revenue money" and "cost money," to put it dramatically, are not automatically the same "money stream." Revenue produces the wherewithal for the costs, of course. But unless management constantly seeks to direct these costs into revenue-producing activities, they will tend to allocate themselves *by drift* into "nothing-producing" activities.

One major reason why managers do not, as a rule, understand this fact is their mistaken identification of *accounting* data and analysis with *economic* data and business analysis.[2] The accountant has to allocate to all products those costs that are not actually and physically tied to a particular unit of production. Today, one way or another, the great bulk of the costs–the 60 percent to 70 percent that are not purchased materials and parts–are, consequently, allocated, rather than truly "direct," costs.

Now the only way the accountant can allocate costs is in a way that is proportionate to volume rather than proportionate to the number of transactions. Thus, $1 million in volume produced in one order–or in one product–carries the same cost as $1 million in volume produced by 1 million individual orders or by 50 different production runs.

Similarly the accountant is concerned with the cost per unit of output rather than with the costs of a product. His focus is on profit margin rather than on profit stream–which is, of course, profit margin multiplied by turnover. Finally, the accountant does not classify costs by the economic activity to which they pertain. Instead, he classifies by organizational or geographic locus (e.g., "manufacturing" or "plant"), or by legal–or legalistic–categories (e.g., "payroll").

I am well aware of the work done on these and related problems of accounting theory and practice–indeed I owe whatever understanding of accounting I have to this work and to the accountants engaged in it. But it will be years before the results of this work will penetrate accounting practice, let alone change the way businessmen use or misuse accounting data.

Rifle Approach

More important than the reasons *why* we have not drawn the right conclusions is: What *are* the right conclusions? What line of action will produce the best possible economic results and performance from the resources available to a business? Let us begin by setting some guidelines:

(1) Economic results require that managers concentrate their efforts on the smallest number of products, product lines, services, customers, markets, distribution channels, end uses, and so on which will produce the largest amount of revenue. Managers must minimize the attention devoted to products which produce primarily costs, because their volume is too small or too splintered.

(2) Economic results require also that staff efforts be concentrated on the very few activities that are capable of producing truly significant business results—with as little staff work and staff effort as possible spent on the others.

(3) Effective cost control requires a similar concentration of work and efforts on those very few areas where improvement in cost performance will have significant impact on business performance and results—that is, on those areas where a relatively *minor* increase in efficiency will produce a *major* increase in economic effectiveness.

(4) Managers must allocate resources, especially *high-grade human resources,* to activities which provide opportunities for high economic results.

Unpardonable Profligacy

No wonder so many businesses did poorly the moment the "seller's market" was over. The wonder, rather, is that they did not do worse. For most businesses—those abroad as well as those in this country—operate in direct opposition to every one of the four well-known rules I have just spelled out.

Instead of product concentration we have product clutter. Remember how it used to be fashionable to attack industry, especially U.S. industry, for its "deadening standardization"? Then, a few years ago, it became fashionable to attack industry for its "planned obsolescence." If only there *were* any validity to either of these charges!

Most businesses—today's large U.S. corporations are perhaps the worst offenders—pride themselves on being willing and able to supply *any* "specialty," to satisfy *any* demand for variety, even to stimulate such demands in the first place. And any number of businesses boast that they never, of their own free will, abandon a product. As a result, most large companies typically end up with thousands of items in their product line—and all too frequently fewer than 20 really "sell." However, these 20 items or less have to contribute revenues to carry the costs of the 9,999 nonsellers.

Indeed, the basic problem of U.S. competitive strength in the world economy today may well be product clutter. If properly costed, the main lines in most of our industries will prove to be fully competitive, despite our high wage rates and our high tax burden. But we fritter away our competitive advantage in the volume products by subsidizing an enormous array of "specialties," of which only a few recover their true cost. This, at least, is what I have found in such industries as steel and aluminum. And in electronics the competitive advantage of the Japanese portable transistor radio rests on little more than the Japanese concentration on a few models in this one line—as against the uncontrolled plethora of barely differentiated models in the U.S. manufacturers' lines.

We are similarly profligate in this country with respect to staff activities. Our motto seems to be, "Let's do a little bit of everything"—personnel research, advanced engineering, customer analysis, international economics, operations research, public relations, and so on. As a result, we build enormous staffs, and yet do not concentrate enough effort in any one area to get very far. Nor do we know what to do to remedy the situation. The common way to control costs is still the one everybody knows to be ineffectual if not destructive: the "across-the-board-cut" by 15 percent. We have not really made a serious attempt to manage resources and pinpoint our efforts. Things are left to drift along.

Three Giant Steps

Criticizing is easy; anyone can find fault. Readers have every right to say, at this point, "Just how can we go about doing a better job of managing?" Even if I had all the answers—and I do not—an article would not be long enough for me to offer a satisfactory reply. This would require a book; and even then every company would *still* have to work out the methods best suited to its own affairs.

So, if readers will bear with me, I will present a series of steps–sketched out only in the lightest of strokes–that I have found to be highly effective in actual business situations, at least as first approaches. Specifically:

Step 1. Analysis

Here the manager has to know the facts. He needs to identify the opportunities and true costs of products, the potential contributions of different staff activities, and the economically significant cost centers.

Step 2. Allocation

Here the manager has to allocate resources according to results anticipated. For this, he needs to know how resources are allocated now, how resources should be allocated in the future to support activities of greatest opportunity, and what steps are necessary to get from what is to what ought to be.

Step 3. Decision

The manager must be prepared to take the most painful step of all–that of deciding on those products, staff activities, or cost areas that breed clutter rather than bring opportunity and results. Naturally, productive resources of any magnitude or potential should never be allocated to these. But which should be abandoned altogether? Which should be maintained at a minimum effort? Which could be changed into major opportunities, and what would it cost to make such a change?

Analyzing the Facts

In the analysis stage, the first job is to take an unsentimental look at the product line. All the standard questions should be asked about each product: its volume, market standing, market outlook, and so on. There is, however, one new key question: What does the product contribute? What does a comparison of its revenue with its true costs show?

In this analysis, revenue should be defined as total sales dollars less costs of purchased materials and supplies. And true costs should be estimated on the basis of this (most probable) assumption–that the real cost of a product is the proportion of the total cost of the business that corresponds to the ratio between the number of transactions (orders, production runs, service calls, and the like) needed to obtain the product's revenue and total number of similar transactions in the business–less, again, materials and parts costs. Since this is cumbersome, let me give a concrete example:

> A company had annual revenues of $68 million, after taking out costs of materials and parts purchased. Total costs of the business–materials and parts excepted–were $56 million.
>
> Product A showed revenues of $12 million a year. It required, however, 24 percent of the total number of transactions–measured in this case by invoices. Its true costs were, therefore, calculated to be $13.5 million a year, which meant a negative contribution, in sharp contrast to the "official" profit margin of almost 12 percent that the accounting figures showed. (This, by the way, is typical for "yesterday's product," which has either lost the main customers or can be held in the market only by uneconomic efforts.)
>
> Product B, by contrast, despite an "unsatisfactory" profit margin of only 3 percent, showed a net revenue contribution of almost $4 million–the largest single contribution to profit. It went in sizable orders to a small number–about 50–of substantial customers.

As the examples show, this analysis looks at *all the products* of a business rather than at one at a time. This by itself is unusual and rarely done.

While the product breakdown is normally the most important and most revealing analysis, customers, markets, distribution channels, and end uses all need to be analyzed similarly in respect to their present and their anticipated contributions.

Staff Contribution

The questions to be asked in this analysis call for managerial judgment rather than for economic data. Here is a list of queries I have found useful:

- In what areas would excellence really have an extraordinary impact on the economic results of our business, to the point where it might transform the economic performance of the entire business?

- In what areas would poor performance threaten to damage economic performance, greatly or at least significantly?

- In what areas would it make little difference whether we perform excellently or poorly?

- What results have been attained by the work done in the area? How do these compare with the results promised or expected?

- What results can realistically be expected for the future–and how far ahead is the future?

Cost Centers

The object here is to isolate those areas of the business where a concentration of cost control efforts will pay off. Rather than describe methods by which this analysis can be carried out, I would like to show the results of an actual study made by a substantial manufacturer of nationally distributed consumer goods (see Figure 1). For convenience, the figures for the various cost centers are given in absolute terms, but each is an approximation. In the actual study, the summary of "total costs," for example, ranged from 90 percent to 94 percent, while other figures had ranges somewhat less extreme.

The only innovation as to methods used by the manufacturer is that "cost" is defined (as it must be when one talks about economics) as what the customer spends on the product. In other words, this analysis looks at the entire economic process as one cost stream, and ignores the accountant's restriction that only those costs which are incurred *within* the legal entity of the business should be considered.

As to results, the important conclusions in this particular example are obvious: where most businesses concentrate their cost control efforts–i.e., on manufacturing–there is not much to be gained except by a real "breakthrough," such as a radically different process. The potentially most productive cost centers either lie *outside* the business, especially in distribution, and require very different treatment from the usual routine of "cost reduction," or they are areas that management rarely even "sees," such as the cost of money.

FIGURE 1.   The consumer's dollar—Where it goes

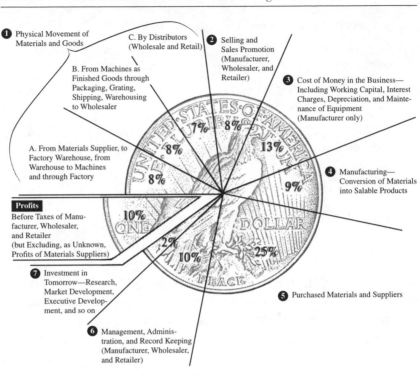

1 Physical Movement of Materials and Goods

C. By Distributors (Wholesale and Retail)

B. From Machines as Finished Goods through Packaging, Grating, Shipping, Warehousing to Wholesaler

A. From Materials Supplier, to Factory Warehouse, from Warehouse to Machines and through Factory

Profits
Before Taxes of Manu-facturer, Wholesaler, and Retailer (but Excluding, as Unknown, Profits of Materials Suppliers)

7 Investment in Tomorrow—Research, Market Development, Executive Develop-ment, and so on

2 Selling and Sales Promotion (Manufacturer, Wholesaler, and Retailer)

3 Cost of Money in the Business—Including Working Capital, Interest Charges, Depreciation, and Mainte-nance of Equipment (Manufacturer only)

4 Manufacturing—Conversion of Materials into Salable Products

5 Purchased Materials and Suppliers

6 Management, Adminis-tration, and Record Keeping (Manufacturer, Wholesaler, and Retailer)

What Ought to Be

The next practical step is that of analyzing how resources are *now* being allocated to product lines, to staff support activities, and to cost centers. The analysis must, of course, be qualitative as well as quantitative. For numbers do not by themselves give the answers to questions like these:

- "Are advertising and promotion dollars going to the right products?"

- "Are capital equipment allocations in accord with realistic expecta-tions for future demands that will be placed on the company?"

- "Is the company's allocation schedule supporting the best people and their activities?"

- "Are these good people deployed full-time on important jobs, or are they spread over so many assignments that they cannot do any one job properly?"

Answers to questions of this sort are often unpleasant, and the remedies they cry out for unpleasant to contemplate. Moving from the allocation stage to the decision stage, consequently, often takes courage.

Priority Decisions

There is only one rule that applies here. Specifically:

> *The areas of greatest potential for opportunity and results are to be given the fullest resource support–in quantity and quality–before the next promising area gets anything.*

Perhaps the area where the toughest and most risky decisions have to be made is that involving products, for the choices are seldom clear-cut and simple. For instance, products will often tend to group themselves into six groups–two with high-contribution potential, three with low- or minus-contribution potential, one in-between. What is fairly typical is a breakdown such as this:

- *Tomorrow's breadwinners*–new products or today's breadwinners modified and improved (rarely today's breadwinners unchanged).

- *Today's breadwinners*–the innovations of yesterday.

- *Products capable of becoming net contributors if something drastic is done;* e.g., converting a good many buyers of "special" variations of limited utility into customers for a new, massive "regular" line. (This is the in-between category.)

- *Yesterday's breadwinners*–typically products with high volume, but badly fragmented into "specials," small orders, and the like, and requiring such massive support as to eat up all they earn, and plenty more. Yet this is–next to the category following–the product class to which the largest and best resources are usually allocated. ("Defensive research" is a common example.)

- *The "also rans"*–typically the high hopes of yesterday that, while they did not work out well, nevertheless did not become outright failures. These are always minus contributors, and practically never become successes no matter how much is poured into them. Yet there is usually far too much managerial and technical ego involved in them to drop them.

- *The failures*–these rarely are a real problem as they tend to liquidate themselves.

This ranking suggests the line that decisions ought to follow. To begin with, the first category should be supplied the necessary resources–and usually a little more than seems necessary. Next, today's breadwinners ought to receive support. By then even a company rich in talent will have to begin to ration. Of the products capable of becoming major contributors, only those should be supported which have either the greatest probability of being reformed, successfully, or would make an *extraordinary* contribution if the reform were accomplished.

And from this point on there just are no high-potential resources available, as a rule–not even in the biggest, best-managed, and most profitable business. The lower half of the third group and groups four, five, and six, either have to produce without any resources and efforts or should be allowed to die. "Yesterday's breadwinner," for instance, often makes a respectable "milch cow" with high yields for a few more years. To expect more and to plow dollars into artificial respiration when the product finally begins to fade is just plain foolish.

The "also rans," who after four or five years of trial and hard work are still runts in the product litter and far below their original expectation, should always be abandoned. There is no greater drain on a business than the product that "almost made it." This is especially true if everyone in the company is convinced that, by quality, by design, or by the cost and difficulty of making it (that is what engineers usually mean when they say "quality"), the pet product is "entitled" to success.

This is part of the last and most crucial "how to do it" requirement: the courage to go through with logical decisions–despite all pleas to give this or that product another chance, and despite all such specious alibis as the accountant's "it absorbs overhead" or the sales manager's "we need a full product line." (Of course, these are not always unfounded alibis, but the burden of proof of every alibi rests with those that plead it.) It would be nice if I did, but unfortunately I know of no procedure or checklist for managerial courage.

Conclusion

What I have sketched out in this article is the manager's real work. As such it requires that he attack the problem of increasing business effectiveness systematically—with a plan of action, with a method of analysis, and with an understanding of the tools he needs.

And while the job to be done may look different in every individual company, one basic truth will always be present: every product and every activity of a business begins to obsolesce as soon as it is started. Every product, every operation, and every activity in a business should, therefore, be put on trial for its life every two or three years. Each should be considered the way we consider a proposal to go into a *new* product, a new operation or activity—complete with budget, capital appropriations request, and so on. One question should be asked of each: "If we were not in this already, would we now go into it?" And if the answer is "no," the next question should be: "How do we get out and how fast?"

The end products of the manager's work are decisions and actions, rather than knowledge and insight. The crucial decision is the allocation of efforts. And no matter how painful, one rule should be adhered to: *in allocating resources, especially human resources of high potential, the needs of those areas which offer great promise must first be satisfied to the fullest extent possible.* If this means that there are no truly productive resources left for a lot of things it would be nice, but not vital, to have or to do, then it is better—much better—to abandon these uses, and not to fritter away high-potential resources or attempt to get results with low-potential ones. This calls for painful decisions, and risky ones. But that, after all, is what managers are paid for.

PART II

The Executive's World

7 The Information Executives Truly Need

E VER SINCE the new data processing tools first emerged 30 or 40 years ago, businesspeople have both overrated and underrated the importance of information in the organization. We–and I include myself–overrated the possibilities to the point where we talked of computer-generated "business models" that could make decisions and might even be able to run much of the business. But we also grossly underrated the new tools; we saw in them the means to do better what executives were already doing to manage their organizations.

Nobody talks of business models making economic decisions anymore. The greatest contribution of our data processing capacity so far has not even been to management. It has been to operations–for example, computer-assisted design or the marvelous software that architects now use to solve structural problems in the buildings they design.

Yet even as we both overestimated and underestimated the new tools, we failed to realize that they would drastically change the *tasks* to be tackled. Concepts and tools, history teaches again and again, are mutually interdependent and interactive. One changes the other. That is now happening to the concept we call a business and to the tools we call information. The new tools enable us–indeed, may force us–to see our businesses differently:

January–February 1995

- as generators of resources, that is, as organizations that can convert business costs into yields;

- as links in an economic chain, which managers need to understand as a whole in order to manage their costs;

- as society's organs for the creation of wealth; and

- as both creatures and creators of a material environment, the area outside the organization in which opportunities and results lie but in which the threats to the success and the survival of every business also originate.

This chapter deals with the tools executives require to generate the information they need. And it deals with the concepts underlying those tools. Some of the tools have been around for a long time, but rarely, if ever, have they been focused on the task of managing a business. Some have to be refashioned; in their present form they no longer work. For some tools that promise to be important in the future, we have so far only the briefest specifications. The tools themselves still have to be designed.

Even though we are just beginning to understand how to use information as a tool, we can outline with high probability the major parts of the information system executives need to manage their businesses. So, in turn, can we begin to understand the concepts likely to underlie the business—call it the redesigned corporation—that executives will have to manage tomorrow.

From Cost Accounting to Yield Control

We may have gone furthest in redesigning both business and information in the most traditional of our information systems: accounting. In fact, many businesses have already shifted from traditional cost accounting to *activity-based costing*. Activity-based costing represents both a different concept of the business process, especially for manufacturers, and different ways of measuring.

Traditional cost accounting, first developed by General Motors 70 years ago, postulates that total manufacturing cost is the sum of the costs of individual operations. Yet the cost that matters for competitiveness and profitability is the cost of the total process, and that is what the new activity-based costing records and makes manageable.

Its basic premise is that manufacturing is an integrated process that starts when supplies, materials, and parts arrive at the plant's loading dock and continues even after the finished product reaches the end user. Service is still a cost of the product, and so is installation, even if the customer pays.

Traditional cost accounting measures what it costs to *do* a task, for example, to cut a screw thread. Activity-based costing also records the cost of *not doing,* such as the cost of machine downtime, the cost of waiting for a needed part or tool, the cost of inventory waiting to be shipped, and the cost of reworking or scrapping a defective part. The costs of not doing, which traditional cost accounting cannot and does not record, often equal and sometimes even exceed the costs of doing. Activity-based costing therefore gives not only much better cost control, but increasingly, it also gives *result control.*

Traditional cost accounting assumes that a certain operation–for example, heat treating–has to be done and that it has to be done where it is being done now. Activity-based costing asks, Does it have to be done? If so, where is it best done? Activity-based costing integrates what were once several activities–value analysis, process analysis, quality management, and costing–into one analysis.

Using that approach, activity-based costing can substantially lower manufacturing costs–in some instances by a full third or more. Its greatest impact, however, is likely to be in services. In most manufacturing companies, cost accounting is inadequate. But service industries–banks, retail stores, hospitals, schools, newspapers, and radio and television stations–have practically no cost information at all.

Activity-based costing shows us why traditional cost accounting has not worked for service companies. It is not because the techniques are wrong. It is because traditional cost accounting makes the wrong assumptions. Service companies cannot start with the cost of individual operations, as manufacturing companies have done with traditional cost accounting. They must start with the assumption that there is only *one* cost: that of the total system. And it is a fixed cost over any given time period. The famous distinction between fixed and variable costs, on which traditional cost accounting is based, does not make much sense in services. Neither does the basic assumption of traditional cost accounting: that capital can be substituted for labor. In fact, in knowledge-based work especially, additional capital investment will likely require more, rather than less, labor. For example, a hospital that buys a new diagnostic tool may have to add four or five people to run it. Other knowledge-based organizations have had to learn the same lesson. But that all costs are fixed over a given time period and that resources cannot be substituted for one another, so that the *total* operation has to be costed—those are precisely the assumptions with which activity-based costing starts. By applying them to services, we are beginning for the first time to get cost information and yield control.

Banks, for instance, have been trying for several decades to apply conventional cost-accounting techniques to their business—that is, to figure the costs of individual operations and services—with almost negligible results. Now they are beginning to ask, Which one *activity* is at the center of costs and of results? The answer: serving the customer. The cost per customer in any major area of banking is a fixed cost. Thus it is the *yield* per customer—both the volume of services a customer uses and the mix of those services—that determines costs and profitability. Retail discounters, especially those in Western Europe, have known that for some time. They assume that once a unit of shelf space is installed, the cost is fixed and management consists of maximizing the yield thereon over a given time span. Their focus on yield control has enabled them to increase profitability despite their low prices and low margins.

Service businesses are only beginning to apply the new costing concepts. In some areas, such as research labs, where productivity is nearly impossible to measure, we may always have to rely on assessment and judgment rather than on measurement. But for most knowledge-based and service work, we should, within 10 to 15 years, have developed reliable tools to measure and manage costs and to relate those costs to results.

Thinking more clearly about costing in services should yield new insights into the costs of getting and keeping customers in all kinds of businesses. If GM, Ford, and Chrysler had used activity-based costing, for example, they would have realized early on the utter futility of their competitive blitzes of the past few years, which offered new-car buyers spectacular discounts and hefty cash rewards. Those promotions actually cost the Big Three automakers enormous amounts of money and, worse, enormous numbers of potential customers. In fact, every one resulted in a nasty drop in market standing. But neither the costs of the special deals nor their negative yields appeared in the companies' conventional cost-accounting figures, so management never saw the damage. Conventional cost accounting shows only the costs of individual manufacturing operations in isolation, and those were not affected by the discounts and rebates in the marketplace. Also, conventional cost accounting does not show the impact of pricing decisions on such things as market share.

Activity-based costing shows—or at least attempts to show—the impact of changes in the costs and yields of every activity on the results of the whole. Had the automakers used it, it soon would have shown the damage done by the discount blitzes. In fact, because the Japanese already use a form of activity-based costing—though still a fairly primitive one—Toyota, Nissan, and Honda knew better than to compete with U.S. automakers through discounts and thus maintained both their market share and their profits.

From Legal Fiction to Economic Reality

Knowing the cost of your operations, however, is not enough. To succeed in the increasingly competitive global market, a company has to know the costs of its entire economic chain and has to work with other members of the chain to manage costs and maximize yield. Companies are therefore beginning to shift from costing only what goes on inside their own organizations to costing the entire economic process, in which even the biggest company is just one link.

The legal entity, the company, is a reality for shareholders, for creditors, for employees, and for tax collectors. But *economically,* it is fiction. Over thirty years ago, the Coca-Cola Company was a franchisor. Independent bottlers manufactured the product. Now the company owns most of its bottling operations in the United States. But Coke drinkers—even those few who know that fact—could not care less. What matters in the marketplace is the economic reality, the costs of the entire process, regardless of who owns what.

Again and again in business history, an unknown company has come from nowhere and in a few short years overtaken the established leaders without apparently even breathing hard. The explanation always given is superior strategy, superior technology, superior marketing, or lean manufacturing. But in every single case, the newcomer also enjoys a tremendous cost advantage, usually about 30 percent. The reason is always the same: the new company knows and manages the costs of the entire economic chain rather than its costs alone.

Toyota is perhaps the best-publicized example of a company that knows and manages the costs of its suppliers and distributors; they are all, of course, members of its *keiretsu*. Through that network, Toyota manages the total cost of making, distributing, and servicing its cars as one cost stream, putting work where it costs the least and yields the most.

Managing the economic cost stream is not a Japanese invention, however, but a U.S. one. It began with the man who designed and built General Motors, William Durant. About 1908, Durant began to buy small, successful automobile companies—Buick, Oldsmobile, Cadillac, Chevrolet—and merged them into his new General Motors Corporation. In 1916, he set up a separate subsidiary called United Motors to buy small, successful parts companies. His first acquisitions included Delco, which held Charles Kettering's patents to the automotive self-starter.

Durant ultimately bought about 20 supplier companies; his last acquisition—in 1919, the year before he was ousted as GM's CEO—was Fisher Body. Durant deliberately brought the parts and accessories makers into the design process of a new automobile model right from the start. Doing so allowed him to manage the total costs of the finished car as one cost stream. In fact, Durant invented the keiretsu.

However, between 1950 and 1960, Durant's keiretsu became an albatross around the company's neck, as unionization imposed higher labor costs on GM's parts divisions than on their independent competitors. As the outside customers, the independent automobile companies such as Packard and Studebaker, which had bought 50 percent of the output of GM's parts divisions, disappeared one by one, GM's control over both the costs and quality of its main suppliers disappeared with them. But for 40 years or more, GM's systems costing gave it an unbeatable advantage over even the most efficient of its competitors, which for most of that time was Studebaker.

Sears, Roebuck and Company was the first to copy Durant's system. In the 1920s, it established long-term contracts with its suppliers and bought minority interests in them. Sears was then able to consult with suppliers as they designed the product and to understand and manage the entire cost stream. That gave the company an unbeatable cost advantage for decades.

In the early 1930s, London-based department store Marks and Spencer copied Sears with the same result. Twenty years later, the Japanese, led by Toyota, studied and copied both Sears and Marks and Spencer. Then in the 1980s, Wal-Mart Stores adapted the approach by allowing suppliers to stock products directly on store shelves, thereby eliminating warehouse inventories and with them nearly one-third of the cost of traditional retailing.

But those companies are still rare exceptions. Although economists have known the importance of costing the entire economic chain since Alfred Marshall wrote about it in the late 1890s, most businesspeople still consider it theoretical abstraction. Increasingly, however, managing the economic cost chain will become a necessity. In their article, "From Lean Production to the Lean Enterprise,"[1] James P. Womack and Daniel T. Jones argue persuasively that executives need to organize and manage not only the cost chain but also everything else–especially corporate strategy and product planning–as one economic whole, regardless of the legal boundaries of individual companies.

A powerful force driving companies toward economic-chain costing will be the shift from cost-led pricing to price-led costing. Traditionally, Western companies have started with costs, put a desired profit margin on top, and arrived at a price. They practiced cost-led pricing. Sears and Marks and Spencer long ago switched to price-led costing, in which the price the customer is willing to pay determines allowable costs, beginning with the design stage. Until recently, those companies were the exceptions. Now price-led costing is becoming the rule. The Japanese first adopted it for their exports. Now Wal-Mart and all the discounters in the United States, Japan, and Europe are practicing price-led costing. It underlies Chrysler's success with its recent models and the success of GM's Saturn. Companies can practice price-led costing, however, only if they know and manage the *entire* cost of the economic chain.

The same ideas apply to outsourcing, alliances, and joint ventures—indeed, to any business structure that is built on partnership rather than control. And such entities, rather than the traditional model of a parent company with wholly owned subsidiaries, are increasingly becoming the models for growth, especially in the global economy.

Still, it will be painful for most businesses to switch to economic-chain costing. Doing so requires uniform or at least compatible accounting systems at companies along the entire chain. Yet each one does its accounting in its own way, and each is convinced that its system is the only possible one. Moreover, economic-chain costing requires information sharing across companies, and even within the same company, people tend to resist information sharing. Despite those challenges, companies can find ways to practice economic-chain costing now, as Procter & Gamble is demonstrating. Using the way Wal-Mart develops close relationships with suppliers as a model, P&G is initiating information sharing and economic-chain management with the 300 large retailers that distribute the bulk of its products worldwide.

Whatever the obstacles, economic-chain costing is going to be done. Otherwise, even the most efficient company will suffer from an increasing cost disadvantage.

Information for Wealth Creation

Enterprises are paid to create wealth, not control costs. But that obvious fact is not reflected in traditional measurements. First-year accounting students are taught that the balance sheet portrays the liquidation value of the enterprise and provides creditors with worst-case information. But enterprises are not normally run to be liquidated. They have to be managed as going concerns, that is, for *wealth creation*. To do that requires information that enables executives to make informed judgments. It requires four sets of diagnostic tools: foundation information, productivity information, competence information, and information about the allocation of scarce resources.

Together, they constitute the executive's tool kit for managing the current business.

Foundation Information

The oldest and most widely used set of diagnostic management tools are cash-flow and liquidity projections and such standard measurements as the ratio between dealers' inventories and sales of new cars; the earnings coverage for the interest payments on a bond issue; and the ratios between receivables outstanding more than six months, total receivables, and sales. Those may be likened to the measurements a doctor takes at a routine physical: weight, pulse, temperature, blood pressure, and urine analysis. If those readings are normal, they do not tell us much. If they are abnormal, they indicate a problem that needs to be identified and treated. Those measurements might be called foundation information.

Productivity Information

The second set of tools for business diagnosis deals with the productivity of key resources. The oldest of them—of World War II vintage—measures the productivity of manual labor. Now we are slowly developing measurements, though still quite primitive ones, for the productivity of knowledge-based and service work. However, measuring only the productivity of workers, whether blue or white collar, no longer gives us adequate information about productivity. We need data on *total-factor productivity*.

That explains the growing popularity of economic value-added analysis (EVA). EVA is based on something we have known for a long time: what we generally call profits, the money left to service equity, is usually not profit at all.[2] Until a business returns a profit that is greater than its cost of capital, it operates at a loss. Never mind that it pays taxes as if it had a genuine profit. The enterprise still returns less to the economy than it devours in resources. It does not cover its full costs unless the reported profit exceeds the cost of capital. Until then, it does not create wealth; it destroys it. By that measurement, incidentally, few U.S. businesses have been profitable since World War II.

By measuring the value added over *all* costs, including the cost of capital, EVA measures, in effect, the productivity of *all* factors of production. It does not, by itself, tell us why a certain product or a certain service does not add value or what to do about it. But it shows us what we need to find out and whether we need to take remedial action. EVA should also be used to find out what works. It does show which product, service, operation, or activity has unusually high productivity and adds unusually high value. Then we should ask ourselves, What can we learn from those successes?

The most recent of the tools used to obtain prductivity information is benchmarking–comparing one's performance with the best performance in the industry or, better yet, with the best anywhere in business. Benchmarking assumes correctly that what one organization does, any other organization can do as well. And it assumes, also correctly, that being at least as good as the leader is a prerequisite to being competitive. Together, EVA and benchmarking provide the diagnostic tools to measure total-factor productivity and to manage it.

Competence Information

A third set of tools deals with competencies. Ever since C. K. Prahalad and Gary Hamel's pathbreaking article, "The Core Competence of the Corporation,"[3] we have known that leadership rests on being able to do something others cannot do at all or find difficult to do even poorly. It rests on core competencies that meld market or customer value with a special ability of the producer or supplier.

Some examples: the ability of the Japanese to miniaturize electronic components, which is based on their 300-year-old artistic tradition of putting landscape paintings on a tiny lacquer box, called an *inro,* and of carving a whole zoo of animals on the even tinier button that holds the box on the wearer's belt, called a *netsuke;* or the almost unique ability GM has had for 80 years to make successful acquisitions; or Marks and Spencer's also unique ability to design packaged and ready-to-eat luxury meals for middle-class budgets. But how does one identify both the core competencies one has already and those the business needs in order to take and maintain a leadership position? How does one find out whether one's core competence is improving or weakening? Or whether it is still the right core competence and what changes it might need?

So far the discussion of core competencies has been largely anecdotal. But a number of highly specialized midsized companies—a Swedish pharmaceutical producer and a U.S. producer of specialty tools, to name two—are developing the methodology to measure and manage core competencies. The first step is to keep careful track of one's own and one's competitors' performances, looking especially for unexpected successes and unexpected poor performance in areas where one should have done well. The successes demonstrate what the market values and will pay for. They indicate where the business enjoys a leadership advantage. The nonsuccesses should be viewed as the first indication either that the market is changing or that the company's competencies are weakening.

That analysis allows for the early recognition of opportunities. For example, by carefully tracking an unexpected success, a U.S. toolmaker found that small Japanese machine shops were buying its high-tech, high-priced tools, even though it had not designed the tools with them in mind or made sales calls to them. That allowed the company to recognize a new core competence: the Japanese were attracted to its products because they were easy to maintain and repair despite their technical complexity. When that insight was applied to designing products, the company gained leadership in the small-plant and machine-shop markets in the United States and Western Europe, huge markets where it had done practically no business before.

Core competencies are different for every organization; they are, so to speak, part of an organization's personality. But every organization—not just businesses—needs one core competence: *innovation.* And every organization needs a way to record and appraise its *innovative performance.* In organizations already doing that—among them several topflight pharmaceutical manufacturers—the starting point is not the company's own performance. It is a careful record of the innovations in the entire field during a given period. Which of them were truly successful? How many of them were ours? Is our performance commensurate with our objectives? With the direction of the market? With our market standing? With our research spending? Are our successful innovations in the areas of greatest growth and opportunity? How many of the truly important innovation opportunities did we miss? Why? Because we did not see them? Or because we saw them but dismissed them? Or because we botched them? And how well do we convert an innovation into a commercial product? A good deal of that, admittedly, is assessment rather than measurement. It raises rather than answers questions, but it raises the right questions.

Resource-Allocation Information

The last area in which diagnostic information is needed to manage the current business for wealth creation is the allocation of scarce resources: capital and performing people. Those two convert into action whatever information management has about its business. They determine whether the enterprise will do well or do poorly.

GM developed the first systematic capital-appropriations process about 70 years ago. Today practically every business has a capital-appropriations process, but few use it correctly. Companies typically measure their proposed capital appropriations by only one or two of the following yardsticks: return on investment, payback period, cash flow, or discounted present value. But we have known for a long time—since the early 1930s—that none of those is *the* right method. To understand a proposed investment, a company needs to look at *all* four. Sixty years ago, that would have required endless number crunching. Now a laptop computer can provide the information within a few minutes. We also have known for 60 years that managers should never look at just one proposed capital appropriation in isolation but should instead choose the projects that show the best ratio between opportunity and risks. That requires a capital-appropriations *budget t*o display the choices—again, something far too many businesses do not do. Most serious, however, is that most capital-appropriations processes do not even ask for two vital pieces of information:

- What will happen if the proposed investment fails to produce the promised results, as do three out of every five? Would it seriously hurt the company, or would it be just a flea bite?

- If the investment is successful—and especially if it is more successful than we expect—what will it commit us to? No one at GM seems to have asked what Saturn's success would commit the company to. As a result, the company may end up killing its own success because of its inability to finance it.

In addition, a capital-appropriations request requires specific deadlines: When should we expect what results? Then the results–successes, near successes, near failures, and failures–need to be reported and analyzed. There is no better way to improve an organization's performance than to measure the results of capital appropriations against the promises and expectations that led to their authorization. How much better off the United States would be today had such feedback on government programs been standard practice for the past 50 years.

Capital, however, is only one key resource of the organization, and it is by no means the scarcest one. The scarcest resources in any organization are performing people. Since World War II, the U.S. military–and so far no one else–has learned to test its placement decisions. It now thinks through what it expects of senior officers before it puts them into key commands. It then appraises their performance against those expectations. And it constantly appraises its own process for selecting senior commanders against the successes and failures of its appointments. In business, by contrast, placement with specific expectations as to what the appointee should achieve and systematic appraisal of the outcome are virtually unknown. In the effort to create wealth, managers need to allocate human resources as purposefully and as thoughtfully as they do capital. And the outcomes of those decisions ought to be recorded and studied as carefully.

Where the Results Are

Those four kinds of information tell us only about the current business. They inform and direct *tactics*. For *strategy,* we need organized information about the environment. Strategy has to be based on information about markets, customers, and noncustomers; about technology in one's own industry and others; about worldwide finance; and about the changing world economy. For that is where the results are. Inside an organization, there are only cost centers. The only profit center is a customer whose check has not bounced.

Major changes also start outside an organization. A retailer may know a great deal about the people who shop at its stores. But no matter how successful it is, no retailer ever has more than a small fraction of the market as its customers; the great majority are non-customers. It is always with noncustomers that basic changes begin and become significant.

At least half the important new technologies that have transformed an industry in the past 50 years came from outside the industry itself. Commercial paper, which has revolutionized finance in the United States, did not originate with the banks. Molecular biology and genetic engineering were not developed by the pharmaceutical industry. Though the great majority of businesses will continue to operate only locally or regionally, they all face, at least potentially, global competition from places they have never even heard of before.

Not all of the needed information about the outside is available, to be sure. There is no information–not even unreliable information–on economic conditions in most of China, for instance, or on legal conditions in most of the successor states to the Soviet empire. But even where information is readily available, many businesses are oblivious to it. Many U.S. companies went into Europe in the 1960s without even asking about labor legislation. European companies have been just as blind and ill informed in their ventures into the United States. A major cause of the Japanese real estate investment debacle in California during the 1990s was the failure to find out elementary facts about zoning and taxes.

A serious cause of business failure is the common assumption that conditions–taxes, social legislation, market preferences, distribution channels, intellectual property rights, and many others–*must* be what we think they are or at least what we think they *should* be. An adequate information system has to include information that makes executives question that assumption. It must lead them to ask the right questions, not just feed them the information they expect. That presupposes first that executives know what information they need. It demands further that they obtain that information on a regular basis. It finally requires that they systematically integrate the information into their decision making.

A few multinationals–Unilever, Coca-Cola, Nestlé, the big Japanese trading companies, and a few big construction companies–have been working hard on building systems to gather and organize outside information. But in general, the majority of enterprises have yet to start the job.

Even big companies, in large part, will have to hire outsiders to help them. To think through what the business needs requires somebody who knows and understands the highly specialized information field. There is far too much information for any but specialists to find their way around. The sources are totally diverse. Companies can generate some of the information themselves, such as information about customers and noncustomers or about the technology in one's own field. But most of what enterprises need to know about the environment is obtainable only from outside sources–from all kinds of data banks and data services, from journals in many languages, from trade associations, from government publications, from World Bank reports and scientific papers, and from specialized studies.

Another reason there is need for outside help is that the information has to be organized so it questions and challenges a company's strategy. To supply data is not enough. The data have to be integrated with strategy, they have to test a company's assumptions, and they must challenge a company's current outlook. One way to do that may be a new kind of software, information tailored to a specific group–say, to hospitals or to casualty insurance companies. The Lexis database supplies such information to lawyers, but it only gives answers; it does not ask questions. What we need are services that make specific suggestions about how to use the information, ask specific questions regarding the users' business and practices, and perhaps provide interactive consultation. Or we might "outsource" the outside-information system. Maybe the most popular provider of the outside-information system, especially for smaller enterprises, will be that "inside outsider," the independent consultant.

Whichever way we satisfy it, the need for information on the environment where the major threats and opportunities are likely to arise will become increasingly urgent.

It may be argued that few of those information needs are new, and that is largely true. Conceptually, many of the new measurements have been discussed for many years and in many places.

What is new is the technical data processing ability. It enables us to do quickly and cheaply what, only a few short years ago, would have been laborious and very expensive. Seventy years ago, the time-and-motion study made traditional cost accounting possible. Computers have now made activity-based cost accounting possible; without them, it would be practically impossible.

But that argument misses the point. What is important is not the tools. It is the concepts behind them. They convert what were always seen as discrete techniques to be used in isolation and for separate purposes into one integrated information system. That system then makes possible business diagnosis, business strategy, and business decisions. That is a new and radically different view of the meaning and purpose of information: as a measurement on which to base future action rather than as a postmortem and a record of what has already happened.

The command-and-control organization that first emerged in the 1870s might be compared to an organism held together by its shell. The corporation that is now emerging is being designed around a skeleton: *information,* both the corporation's new integrating system and its articulation.

Our traditional mind-set—even if we use sophisticated mathematical techniques and impenetrable sociological jargon—has always somehow perceived business as buying cheap and selling dear. The new approach defines a business as the organization that adds value and creates wealth.

8 The Coming of the New Organization

T HE TYPICAL large business 20 years hence will have fewer than half the levels of management of its counterpart today, and no more than a third of the managers. In its structure, and in its management problems and concerns, it will bear little resemblance to the typical manufacturing company, circa 1950, which our text-books still consider the norm. Instead it is far more likely to resemble organizations that neither the practicing manager nor the manage-ment scholar pays much attention to today: the hospital, the univer-sity, the symphony orchestra. For like them, the typical business will be knowledge-based, an organization composed largely of spe-cialists who direct and discipline their own performance through organized feedback from colleagues, customers, and headquarters. For this reason, it will be what I call an information-based organiza-tion.

Businesses, especially large ones, have little choice but to become information-based. Demographics, for one, demands the shift. The center of gravity in employment is moving fast from manual and clerical workers to knowledge workers who resist the command-and-control model that business took from the military 100 years ago. Economics also dictates change, especially the need for large

January–February 1988

businesses to innovate and to be entrepreneurs. But above all, information technology demands the shift.

Advanced data-processing technology isn't necessary to create an information-based organization, of course. As we shall see, the British built just such an organization in India when "information technology" meant the quill pen, and barefoot runners were the "telecommunications" systems. But as advanced technology becomes more and more prevalent, we have to engage in analysis and diagnosis—that is, in "information"—even more intensively or risk being swamped by the data we generate.

So far most computer users still use the new technology only to do faster what they have always done before, crunch conventional numbers. But as soon as a company takes the first tentative steps from data to information, its decision processes, management structure, and even the way its work gets done begin to be transformed. In fact, this is already happening, quite fast, in a number of companies throughout the world.

W<small>E CAN</small> readily see the first step in this transformation process when we consider the impact of computer technology on capital-investment decisions. We have known for a long time that there is no one right way to analyze a proposed capital investment. To understand it we need at least six analyses: the expected rate of return; the payout period and the investment's expected productive life; the discounted present value of all returns through the productive lifetime of the investment; the risk in not making the investment or deferring it; the cost and risk in case of failure; and finally, the opportunity cost. Every accounting student is taught these concepts. But before the advent of data-processing capacity, the actual analyses would have taken man-years of clerical toil to complete. Now anyone with a spreadsheet should be able to do them in a few hours.

The availability of this information transforms the capital-investment analysis from opinion into diagnosis, that is, into the rational weighing of alternative assumptions. Then the information transforms the capital-investment decision from an opportunistic, financial decision governed by the numbers into a business decision based on the probability of alternative strategic assumptions. So the decision both presupposes a business strategy and challenges that strategy and its assumptions. What was once a budget exercise becomes an analysis of policy.

The second area that is affected when a company focuses its data-processing capacity on producing information is its organization structure. Almost immediately, it becomes clear that both the number of management levels and the number of managers can be sharply cut. The reason is straightforward: it turns out that whole layers of management neither make decisions nor lead. Instead, their main, if not their only, function is to serve as "relays"–human boosters for the faint, unfocused signals that pass for communication in the traditional pre-information organization.

One of America's largest defense contractors made this discovery when it asked what information its top corporate and operating managers needed to do their jobs. Where did it come from? What form was it in? How did it flow? The search for answers soon revealed that whole layers of management–perhaps as many as 6 out of a total of 14–existed only because these questions had not been asked before. The company had had data galore. But it had always used its copious data for control rather than for information.

Information is data endowed with relevance and purpose. Converting data into information thus requires knowledge. And knowledge, by definition, is specialized. (In fact, truly knowledgeable people tend toward overspecialization, whatever their field, precisely because there is always so much more to know.)

The information-based organization requires far more specialists overall than the command-and-control companies we are accustomed to. Moreover, the specialists are found in operations, not as corporate headquarters. Indeed, the operating organization tends to become an organization of specialists of all kinds.

Information-based organizations need central operating work such as legal counsel, public relations, and labor relations as much as ever. But the need for service staffs–that is, for people without operating responsibilities who only advise, counsel, or coordinate–shrinks drastically. In its *central* management, the information-based organization needs few, if any, specialists.

Because of its flatter structure, the large, information-based organization will more closely resemble the businesses of a century ago than today's big companies. Back then, however, all the knowledge, such as it was, lay with the very top people. The rest were helpers or hands, who mostly did the same work and did as they were told. In the information-based organization, the knowledge will be primarily at the bottom, in the minds of the specialists who do different work and direct themselves. So today's typical organization in which knowledge tends to be concentrated in service staffs, perched rather insecurely between top management and the operating people, will likely be labeled a phase, an attempt to infuse knowledge from the top rather than obtain information from below.

Finally, a good deal of work will be done differently in the information-based organization. Traditional departments will serve as guardians of standards, as centers for training and the assignment of specialists; they won't be where the work gets done. That will happen largely in task-focused teams.

This change is already under way in what used to be the most clearly defined of all departments—research. In pharmaceuticals, in telecommunications, in papermaking, the traditional *sequence* of research, development, manufacturing, and marketing is being replaced by *synchrony*: specialists from all these functions work together as a team, from the inception of research to a product's establishment in the market.

How task forces will develop to tackle other business opportunities and problems remains to be seen. I suspect, however, that the need for a task force, its assignment, its composition, and its leadership will have to be decided on case by case. So the organization that will be developed will go beyond the matrix and may indeed be quite different from it. One thing is clear, though: it will require greater self-discipline and even greater emphasis on individual responsibility for relationships and for communications.

T O S A Y that information technology is transforming business enterprises is simple. What this transformation will require of companies and top managements is much harder to decipher. That is why I find it helpful to look for clues in other kinds of information-based organizations, such as the hospital, the symphony orchestra, and the British administration in India.

A fair-sized hospital of about 400 beds will have a staff of several hundred physicians and 1,200 to 1,500 paramedics divided among some 60 medical and paramedical specialties. Each specialty has its own knowledge, its own training, its own language. In each specialty, especially the paramedical ones like the clinical lab and physical therapy, there is a head person who is a working specialist rather than a full-time manager. The head of each specialty reports directly to the top, and there is little middle management. A good deal of the work is done in ad hoc teams as required by an individual patient's diagnosis and condition.

A large symphony orchestra is even more instructive, since for some works there may be a few hundred musicians on stage playing together. According to organization theory then, there should be several group vice president conductors and perhaps a half-dozen division VP conductors. But that's not how it works. There is only the conductor-CEO—and every one of the musicians plays directly to that person without an intermediary. And each is a high-grade specialist, indeed an artist.

But the best example of a large and successful information-based organization, and one without any middle management at all, is the British civil administration in India.[1]

The British ran the Indian subcontinent for 200 years, from the middle of the eighteenth century through World War II, without making any fundamental changes in organization structure or administrative policy. The Indian civil service never had more than 1,000 members to administer the vast and densely populated subcontinent—a tiny fraction (at most 1 percent) of the legions of Confucian mandarins and palace eunuchs employed next door to administer a not-much-more populous China. Most of the Britishers were quite young; a 30-year-old was a survivor, especially in the early years. Most lived alone in isolated outposts with the nearest countryman a day or two of travel away, and for the first hundred years there was no telegraph or railroad.

The organization structure was totally flat. Each district officer reported directly to the "Coo," the provincial political secretary. And since there were nine provinces, each political secretary had at least

100 people reporting directly to him, many times what the doctrine of the span of control would allow. Nevertheless, the system worked remarkably well, in large part because it was designed to ensure that each of its members had the information he needed to do his job.

Each month the district officer spent a whole day writing a full report to the political secretary in the provincial capital. He discussed each of his principal tasks–there were only four, each clearly delineated. He put down in detail what he had expected would happen with respect to each of them, what actually did happen, and why, if there was a discrepancy, the two differed. Then he wrote down what he expected would happen in the ensuing month with respect to each key task and what he was going to do about it, asked questions about policy, and commented on long-term opportunities, threats, and needs. In turn, the political secretary "minuted" every one of those reports–that is, he wrote back a full comment.

ON THE BASIS of these examples, what can we say about the requirements of the information-based organization? And what are its management problems likely to be? Let's look first at the requirements. Several hundred musicians and their CEO, the conductor, can play together because they all have the same score. It tells both flutist and timpanist what to play and when. And it tells the conductor what to expect from each and when. Similarly, all the specialists in the hospital share a common mission: the care and cure of the sick. The diagnosis is their "score"; it dictates specific action for the X-ray lab, the dietitian, the physical therapist, and the rest of the medical team.

Information-based organizations, in other words, require clear, simple, common objectives that translate into particular actions. At the same time, however, as these examples indicate, information-based organizations also need concentration on one objective or, at most, on a few.

Because the "players" in an information-based organization are specialists, they cannot be told how to do their work. There are probably few orchestra conductors who could coax even one note out of a French horn, let alone show the horn player how to do it.

But the conductor can focus the horn player's skill and knowledge on the musicians' joint performance. And this focus is what the leaders of an information-based business must be able to achieve.

Yet a business has no "score" to play by except the score it writes as it plays. And whereas neither a first-rate performance of a symphony nor a miserable one will change what the composer wrote, the performance of a business continually creates new and different scores against which its performance is assessed. So an information-based business must be structured around goals that clearly state management's performance expectations for the enterprise and for each part and specialist and around organized feedback that compares results with these performance expectations so that every member can exercise self-control.

The other requirement of an information-based organization is that everyone take information responsibility. The bassoonist in the orchestra does so every time she plays a note. Doctors and paramedics work with an elaborate system of reports and an information center, the nurse's station on the patient's floor. The district officer in India acted on this responsibility every time he filed a report.

The key to such a system is that everyone asks: Who in this organization depends on me for what information? And on whom, in turn, do I depend? Each person's list will always include superiors and subordinates. But the most important names on it will be those of colleagues, people with whom one's primary relationship is coordination. The relationship of the internist, the surgeon, and the anesthesiologist is one example. But the relationship of a biochemist, a pharmacologist, the medical director in charge of clinical testing, and a marketing specialist in a pharmaceutical company is no different. It, too, requires each party to take the fullest information responsibility.

Information responsibility to others is increasingly understood, especially in middle-sized companies. But information responsibility to oneself is still largely neglected. That is, everyone in an organization should constantly be thinking through what information he or she needs to do the job and to make a contribution.

This may well be the most radical break with the way even the most highly computerized businesses are still being run today. There, people either assume the more data, the more information—

which was a perfectly valid assumption yesterday when data were scarce, but leads to data overload and information blackout now that they are plentiful. Or they believe that information specialists know what data executives and professionals need in order to have information. But information specialists are tool makers. They can tell us what tool to use to hammer upholstery nails into a chair. We need to decide whether we should be upholstering a chair at all.

Executives and professional specialists need to think through what information is for them, what data they need: first, to know what they are doing; then, to be able to decide what they should be doing; and finally, to appraise how well they are doing. Until this happens MIS departments are likely to remain cost centers rather than become the result centers they could be.

Most large businesses have little in common with the examples we have been looking at. Yet to remain competitive—maybe even to survive—they will have to convert themselves into information-based organizations, and fairly quickly. They will have to change old habits and acquire new ones. And the more successful a company has been, the more difficult and painful this process is apt to be. It will threaten the jobs, status, and opportunities of a good many people in the organization, especially the long-serving, middle-aged people in middle management who tend to be the least mobile and to feel most secure in their work, their positions, their relationships, and their behavior.

The information-based organization will also pose its own special management problems. I see as particularly critical:

1. Developing rewards, recognition, and career opportunities for specialists.

2. Creating unified vision in an organization of specialists.

3. Devising the management structure for an organization of task forces.

4. Ensuring the supply, preparation, and testing of top management people.

Bassoonists presumably neither want nor expect to be anything but bassoonists. Their career opportunities consist of moving from second bassoon to first bassoon and perhaps of moving from a second-rank orchestra to a better, more prestigious one. Similarly, many medical technologists neither expect nor want to be anything but medical technologists. Their career opportunities consist of a fairly good chance of moving up to senior technician, and a very slim chance of becoming lab director. For those who make it to lab director, about 1 out of every 25 or 30 technicians, there is also the opportunity to move to a bigger, richer hospital. The district officer in India had practically no chance for professional growth except possibly to be relocated, after a three-year stint, to a bigger district.

Opportunities for specialists in an information-based business organization should be more plentiful than they are in an orchestra or hospital, let alone in the Indian civil service. But as in these organizations, they will primarily be opportunities for advancement within the specialty, and for limited advancement at that. Advancement into "management" will be the exception, for the simple reason that there will be far fewer middle-management positions to move into. This contrasts sharply with the traditional organization where, except in the research lab, the main line of advancement in rank is out of the specialty and into general management.

More than 30 years ago General Electric tackled this problem by creating "parallel opportunities" for "individual professional contributors." Many companies have followed this example. But professional specialists themselves have largely rejected it as a solution. To them—and to their management colleagues—the only meaningful opportunities are promotions into management. And the prevailing compensation structure in practically all businesses reinforces this attitude because it is heavily biased towards managerial positions and titles.

There are no easy answers to this problem. Some help may come from looking at large law and consulting firms, where even the most senior partners tend to be specialists, and associates who will not make partner are outplaced fairly early on. But whatever scheme is eventually developed will work only if the values and compensation structure of business are drastically changed.

The second challenge that management faces is giving its organization of specialists a common vision, a view of the whole.

In the Indian civil service, the district officer was expected to see the "whole" of his district. But to enable him to concentrate on it, the government services that arose one after the other in the nineteenth century (forestry, irrigation, the archaeological survey, public health and sanitation, roads) were organized outside the administrative structure, and had virtually no contact with the district officer. This meant that the district officer became increasingly isolated from the activities that often had the greatest impact on—and the greatest importance for—his district. In the end, only the provincial government or the central government in Delhi had a view of the "whole," and it was an increasingly abstract one at that.

A business simply cannot function this way. It needs a view of the whole and a focus on the whole to be shared among a great many of its professional specialists, certainly among the senior ones. And yet it will have to accept, indeed will have to foster, the pride and professionalism of its specialists—if only because, in the absence of opportunities to move into middle management, their motivation must come from that pride and professionalism.

One way to foster professionalism, of course, is through assignments to task forces. And the information-based business will use more and more smaller self-governing units, assigning them tasks tidy enough for "a good man to get his arms around," as the old phrase has it. But to what extent should information-based businesses rotate performing specialists out of their specialties and into new ones? And to what extent will top management have to accept as its top priority making and maintaining a common vision across professional specialties?

Heavy reliance on task-force teams assuages one problem. But it aggravates another: the management structure of the information-based organization. Who will the business's managers be? Will they be task-force leaders? Or will there be a two-headed monster—a specialist structure, comparable, perhaps, to the way attending physicians function in a hospital, and an administrative structure of task-force leaders?

The decisions we face on the role and function of the task-force leaders are risky and controversial. Is theirs a permanent assignment, analagous to the job of the supervisory nurse in the hospital? Or is it a function of the task that changes as the task does? Is it an assignment or a position? Does it carry any rank at all? And if it does, will the task-force leaders become in time what the product managers have been at Procter & Gamble: the basic units of management and the company's field officers? Might the task-force leaders eventually replace department heads and vice presidents?

Signs of every one of these developments exist, but there is neither a clear trend nor much understanding as to what each entails. Yet each would give rise to a different organizational structure from any we are familiar with.

Finally, the toughest problem will probably be to ensure the supply, preparation, and testing of top management people. This is, of course, an old and central dilemma as well as a major reason for the general acceptance of decentralization in large businesses in the last 40 years. But the existing business organization has a great many middle-management positions that are supposed to prepare and test a person. As a result, there are usually a good many people to choose from when filling a senior management slot. With the number of middle-management positions sharply cut, where will the information-based organization's top executives come from? What will be their preparation? How will they have been tested?

Decentralization into autonomous units will surely be even more critical than it is now. Perhaps we will even copy the German *Gruppe* in which the decentralized units are set up as separate companies with their own top managements. The Germans use this model precisely because of their tradition of promoting people in their specialties, especially in research and engineering; if they did not have available commands in near-independent subsidiaries to put people in, they would have little opportunity to train and test their most promising professionals. These subsidiaries are thus somewhat like the farm teams of a major-league baseball club.

We may also find that more and more top management jobs in big companies are filled by hiring people away from smaller companies. This is the way that major orchestras get their conductors—a young conductor earns his or her spurs in a small orchestra or opera house, only to be hired away by a larger one. And the heads of a good many large hospitals have had similar careers.

Can business follow the example of the orchestra and hospital where top management has become a separate career? Conductors and hospital administrators come out of courses in conducting or schools of hospital administration respectively. We see something of this sort in France, where large companies are often run by men who have spent their entire previous careers in government service. But in most countries this would be unacceptable to the organization (only France has the *mystique* of the *grandes écoles*). And even in France, businesses, especially large ones, are becoming too demanding to be run by people without firsthand experience and a proven success record.

Thus the entire top management process–preparation, testing, succession–will become even more problematic than it already is. There will be a growing need for experienced businesspeople to go back to school. And business schools will surely need to work out what successful professional specialists must know to prepare themselves for high-level positions as *business* executives and *business* leaders.

S INCE modern business enterprise first arose, after the Civil War in the United States and the Franco-Prussian War in Europe, there have been two major evolutions in the concept and structure of organizations. The first took place in the ten years between 1895 and 1905. It distinguished management from ownership and established management as work and task in its own right. This happened first in Germany, when Georg Siemens, the founder and head of Germany's premier bank, Deutsche Bank, saved the electrical apparatus company his cousin Werner had founded after Werner's sons and heirs had mismanaged it into near collapse. By threatening to cut off the bank's loans, he forced his cousins to turn the company's management over to professionals. A little later, J. P. Morgan, Andrew Carnegie, and John D. Rockefeller, Sr. followed suit in their massive restructurings of U.S. railroads and industries.

The second evolutionary change took place 20 years later. The development of what we still see as the modern corporation began with Pierre S. du Pont's restructuring of his family company in the early twenties and continued with Alfred P. Sloan's redesign of

General Motors a few years later. This introduced the command-and-control organization of today, with its emphasis on decentralization, central service staffs, personnel management, the whole apparatus of budgets and controls, and the important distinction between policy and operations. This stage culminated in the massive reorganization of General Electric in the early 1950s, an action that perfected the model most big businesses around the world (including Japanese organizations) still follow.[2]

Now we are entering a third period of change: the shift from the command-and-control organization, the organization of departments and divisions, to the information-based organization, the organization of knowledge specialists. We can perceive, though perhaps only dimly, what this organization will look like. We can identify some of its main characteristics and requirements. We can point to central problems of values, structure, and behavior. But the job of actually building the information-based organization is still ahead of us–it is the managerial challenge of the future.

9 The New Society
of Organizations

E VERY FEW hundred years throughout Western history, a sharp transformation has occurred. In a matter of decades, society altogether rearranges itself—its world view, its basic values, its social and political structures, its arts, its key institutions. Fifty years later a new world exists. And the people born into that world cannot even imagine the world in which their grandparents lived and into which their own parents were born.

Our age is such a period of transformation. Only this time the transformation is not confined to Western society and Western history. Indeed, one of the fundamental changes is that there is no longer a "Western" history or a "Western" civilization. There is only world history and world civilization.

Whether this transformation began with the emergence of the first non-Western country, Japan, as a great economic power or with the first computer—that is, with information—is moot. My own candidate would be the GI Bill of Rights, which gave every American soldier returning from World War II the money to attend a university, something that would have made absolutely no sense only 30 years earlier at the end of World War I. The GI Bill of Rights and the enthusiastic response to it on the part of America's veterans signaled the shift to a knowledge society.

In this society, knowledge is *the* primary resource for individuals and for the economy overall. Land, labor, and capital—the econo-

September–October 1992

mist's traditional factors of production—do not disappear, but they become secondary. They can be obtained, and obtained easily, provided there is specialized knowledge. At the same time, however, specialized knowledge by itself produces nothing. It can become productive only when it is integrated into a task. And that is why the knowledge society is also a society of organizations: the purpose and function of every organization, business and non-business alike, is the integration of specialized knowledges into a common task.

If history is any guide, this transformation will not be completed until 2010 or 2020. Therefore, it is risky to try to foresee in every detail the world that is emerging. But what new questions will arise and where the big issues will lie we can, I believe, already discover with a high degree of probability.

In particular, we already know the central tensions and issues that confront the society of organizations: the tension created by the community's need for stability and the organization's need to destabilize; the relationship between individual and organization and the responsibilities of one to another; the tension that arises from the organization's need for autonomy and society's stake in the Common Good; the rising demand for socially responsible organizations; the tension between specialists with specialized knowledges and performance as a team. All of these will be central concerns, especially in the developed world, for years to come. They will not be resolved by pronunciamiento or philosophy or legislation. They will be resolved where they originate: in the individual organization and in the manager's office.

S OCIETY, community, and family are all conserving institutions. They try to maintain stability and to prevent, or at least to slow, change. But the modern organization is a destabilizer. It must be organized for innovation and innovation, as the great Austro-American economist Joseph Schumpeter said, is "creative destruction." And it must be organized for the systematic abandonment of whatever is established, customary, familiar, and comfortable, whether that is a product, service, or process; a set of skills; human and social relationships; or the organization itself. In short, it must be organized for constant change. The organization's function is to put knowledge to work—on tools, products, and processes; on the design of work; on knowledge itself. It is the nature of knowledge that it changes fast and that today's certainties always become tomorrow's absurdities.

Skills change slowly and infrequently. If an ancient Greek stone-cutter came back to life today and went to work in a stone mason's yard, the only change of significance would be the design he was asked to carve on the tombstones. The tools he would use are the same, only now they have electric batteries in the handles. Through-out history, the craftsman who had learned a trade after five or seven years of apprenticeship had learned, by age eighteen or nineteen, everything he would ever need to use during his lifetime. In the society of organizations, however, it is safe to assume that anyone with any knowledge will have to acquire new knowledge every four or five years or become obsolete.

This is doubly important because the changes that affect a body of knowledge most profoundly do not, as a rule, come out of its own domain. After Gutenberg first used movable type, there was practically no change in the craft of printing for 400 years—until the steam engine came in. The greatest challenge to the railroad came not from changes in railroading but from the automobile, the truck, and the airplane. The pharmaceutical industry is being profoundly changed today by knowledge coming from genetics and microbiol-ogy, disciplines that few biologists had heard of 40 years ago.

And it is by no means only science or technology that creates new knowledge and makes old knowledge obsolete. Social innovation is equally important and often more important than scientific innova-tion. Indeed, what triggered the present worldwide crisis in that proudest of nineteenth-century institutions, the commercial bank, was not the computer or any other technological change. It was the discovery by nonbankers that an old but hitherto rather obscure financial instrument, commercial paper, could be used to finance companies and would thus deprive the banks of the business on which they had held a monopoly for 200 years and which gave them most of their income: the commercial loan. The greatest change of all is probably that in the last 40 years purposeful innovation—both technical and social—has itself become an organized discipline that is both teachable and learnable.

Nor is rapid knowledge-based change confined to business, as many still believe. No organization in the 50 years since World War II has changed more than the U.S. military. Uniforms have remained the same. Titles of rank have remained the same. But weapons have changed completely, as the Gulf War of 1991 dramatically demonstrated; military doctrines and concepts have changed even more drastically, as have the armed services' organizational structures, command structures, relationships, and responsibilities.

Similarly, it is a safe prediction that in the next 50 years, schools and universities will change more and more drastically than they have since they assumed their present form more than 300 years ago when they reorganized themselves around the printed book. What will force these changes is, in part, new technology, such as computers, videos, and telecasts via satellite; in part the demands of a knowledge-based society in which organized learning must become a lifelong process for knowledge workers; and in part new theory about how human beings learn.

FOR managers, the dynamics of knowledge impose one clear imperative: every organization has to build the management of change into its very structure.

On the one hand, this means every organization has to prepare for the abandonment of everything it does. Managers have to learn to ask every few years of every process, every product, every procedure, every policy: "If we did not do this already, would we go into it now knowing what we now know?" If the answer is no, the organization has to ask, "So what do we do now?" And it has to *do* something, and not say, "Let's make another study." Indeed, organizations increasingly will have to *plan* abandonment rather than try to prolong the life of a successful product, policy, or practice–something that so far only a few large Japanese companies have faced up to.

On the other hand, every organization must devote itself to creating the new. Specifically, every management has to draw on three systematic practices. The first is continuing improvement of everything the organization does, the process the Japanese call *kaizen*. Every artist throughout history has practiced kaizen, or organized, continuous self-improvement. But so far only the Japanese–perhaps because of their Zen tradition–have embodied it in the daily life and work of their business organizations (although not in their singularly change-resistant universities). The aim of kaizen is to improve a product or service so that it becomes a truly different product or service in two or three years' time.

Second, every organization will have to learn to exploit its knowledge, that is, to develop the next generation of applications from its own successes. Again, Japanese businesses have done the best with this endeavor so far, as demonstrated by the success of the consumer electronics manufacturers in developing one new product after another from the same American invention, the tape recorder. But successful exploitation of their successes is also one of the strengths of the fast-growing American pastoral churches.

Finally, every organization will have to learn to innovate–and innovation can now be organized and must be organized–as a systematic process. And then, of course, one comes back to abandonment, and the process starts all over. Unless this is done, the knowledge-based organization will very soon find itself obsolescent, losing performance capacity and with it the ability to attract and hold the skilled and knowledgeable people on whom its performance depends.

The need to organize for change also requires a high degree of decentralization. That is because the organization must be structured to make decisions quickly. And those decisions must be based on closeness–to performance, to the market, to technology, and to all the many changes in society, the environment, demographics, and knowledge that provide opportunities for innovation if they are seen and utilized.

All this implies, however, that the organizations of the post-capitalist society must constantly upset, disorganize, and destabilize the community. They must change the demand for skills and knowledges: just when every technical university is geared up to teach physics, organizations need geneticists. Just when bank employees are most proficient in credit analysis, they will need to be investment counselors. But also, businesses must be free to close factories on which local communities depend for employment or to replace grizzled model makers who have spent years learning their craft with 25-year-old whiz kids who know computer simulation.

Similarly, hospitals must be able to move the delivery of babies into a free-standing birthing center when the knowledge base and technology of obstetrics change. And we must be able to close a hospital altogether when changes in medical knowledge, technology, and practice make a hospital with fewer than 200 beds both uneconomical and incapable of giving first-rate care. For a hospital—or a school or any other community organization—to discharge its social function we must be able to close it down, no matter how deeply rooted in the local community it is and how much beloved, if changes in demographics, technology, or knowledge set new prerequisites for performance.

But every one of such changes upsets the community, disrupts it, deprives it of continuity. Every one is "unfair." Every one destabilizes.

EQUALLY disruptive is another fact of organizational life: the modern organization must be *in* a community but cannot be *of* it. An organization's members live in a particular place, speak its language, send their children to its schools, vote, pay taxes, and need to feel at home there. Yet the organization cannot submerge itself in the community nor subordinate itself to the community's ends. Its "culture" has to transcend community.

It is the nature of the task, not the community in which the task is being performed, that determines the culture of an organization. The American civil servant, though totally opposed to communism, will understand immediately what a Chinese colleague tells him about bureaucratic intrigues in Beijing. But he would be totally baffled in his own Washington, D.C. if he were to sit in on a discussion of the next week's advertising promotions by the managers of the local grocery chain.

To perform its task the organization has to be organized and managed the same way as others of its type. For example, we hear a great deal about the differences in management between Japanese and American companies. But a large Japanese company functions very much like a large American company; and both function very much like a large German or British company. Likewise, no one will ever doubt that he or she is in a hospital, no matter where the hospital is located. The same holds true for schools and universities, for labor unions and research labs, for museums and opera houses, for astronomical observatories and large farms.

In addition, each organization has a value system that is determined by its task. In every hospital in the world, health care is considered the ultimate good. In every school in the world, learning is considered the ultimate good. In every business in the world, production and distribution of goods or services is considered the ultimate good. For the organization to perform to a high standard, its members must believe that what it is doing is, in the last analysis, the one contribution to community and society on which all others depend.

In its culture, therefore, the organization will always transcend the community. If an organization's culture and the values of its community clash, the organization must prevail—or else it will not make its social contribution. "Knowledge knows no boundaries," says an old proverb. There has been a "town and gown" conflict ever since the first university was established more than 750 years ago. But such a conflict—between the autonomy the organization needs in order to perform and the claims of the community, between the values of the organization and those of the community, between the decisions facing the organization and the interests of the community—is inherent in the society of organizations.

T H E issue of social responsibility is also inherent in the society of organizations. The modern organization has and must have social power—and a good deal of it. It needs power to make decisions about people: whom to hire, whom to fire, whom to promote. It needs power to establish the rules and disciplines required to produce results: for example, the assignment of jobs and tasks and the establishment of working hours. It needs power to decide which factories to build where and which factories to close. It needs power to set prices, and so on.

And nonbusinesses have the greatest social power—far more, in fact, than business enterprises. Few organizations in history were ever granted the power the university has today. Refusing to admit a student or to grant a student the diploma is tantamount to debarring that person from careers and opportunities. Similarly, the power of the American hospital to deny a physician admitting privileges is the power to exclude that physician from the practice of medicine. The labor union's power over admission to apprenticeship or its control of access to employment in a "closed shop," where only union members can be hired, gives the union tremendous social power.

The power of the organization can be restrained by political power. It can be made subject to due process and to review by the courts. But it must be exercised by individual organizations rather than by political authorities. This is why post-capitalist society talks so much about social responsibilities of the organization.

It is futile to argue, as Milton Friedman, the American economist and Nobel-laureate does, that a business has only one responsibility: economic performance. Economic performance is the *first* responsibility of a business. Indeed, a business that does not show a profit at least equal to its cost of capital is irresponsible; it wastes society's resources. Economic performance is the base without which a business cannot discharge any other responsibilities, cannot be a good employer, a good citizen, a good neighbor. But economic performance is not the *only* responsibility of a business any more than educational performance is the only responsibility of a school or health care the only responsibility of a hospital.

Unless power is balanced by responsibility, it becomes tyranny. Furthermore, without responsibility power always degenerates into nonperformance, and organizations must perform. So the demand for socially responsible organizations will not go away but rather widen.

Fortunately, we also know, if only in rough outline, how to answer the problem of social responsibility. Every organization must assume full responsibility for its impact on employees, the environment, customers, and whomever and whatever it touches. That is its social responsibility. But we also know that society will increasingly look to major organizations, for-profit and nonprofit alike, to tackle major social ills. And there we had better be watchful because good intentions are not always socially responsible. It is irresponsible for an organization to accept—let alone to pursue—responsibilities that would impede its capacity to perform its main task and mission or to act where it has no competence.

Organization has become an everyday term. Everybody nods when somebody says, "In our organization, everything should revolve around the customer" or "In this organization, they never forget a mistake." And most, if not all, social tasks in every developed country are performed in and by an organization of one kind or another. Yet no one in the United States—or anyplace else—talked of "organizations" until after World War II. *The Concise Oxford Dictionary* did not even list the term in its current meaning in the 1950 edition. It is only the emergence of management since World War II, what I call the "Management Revolution," that has allowed us to see that the organization is discrete and distinct from society's other institutions.

Unlike "community," "society," or "family," organizations are purposefully designed and always specialized. Community and society are defined by the bonds that hold their members together, whether they be language, culture, history, or locality. An organization is defined by its task. The symphony orchestra does not attempt to cure the sick; it plays music. The hospital takes care of the sick but does not attempt to play Beethoven.

Indeed, an organization is effective only if it concentrates on one task. Diversification destroys the performance capacity of an organization, whether it is a business, a labor union, a school, a hospital, a community service, or a house of worship. Society and community must be multidimensional; they are environments. An organization is a tool. And as with any other tool, the more specialized it is, the greater its capacity to perform its given task.

Because the modern organization is composed of specialists, each with his or her own narrow area of expertise, its mission must be crystal clear. The organization must be single-minded, or its members will become confused. They will follow their own specialty rather than apply it to the common task. They will each define "results" in terms of their own specialty and impose its values on the organization. Only a focused and common mission will hold the organization together and enable it to produce. Without such a mission, the organization will soon lose credibility and, with it, its ability to attract the very people it needs to perform.

It can be all too easy for managers to forget that joining an organization is always voluntary. De facto there may be little choice. But even where membership is all but compulsory—as membership in the Catholic church was in all the countries of Europe for many centuries for all but a handful of Jews and Gypsies—the fiction of voluntary choice is always carefully maintained: the godfather at the infant's baptism pledges the child's voluntary acceptance of membership in the church.

Likewise, it may be difficult to leave an organization—the Mafia, for instance, a big Japanese company, the Jesuit order. But it is always possible. And the more an organization becomes an organization of knowledge workers, the easier it is to leave it and move elsewhere. Therefore, an organization is always in competition for its most essential resource: qualified, knowledgeable people.

ALL organizations now say routinely, "People are our greatest asset." Yet few practice what they preach, let alone truly believe it. Most still believe, though perhaps not consciously, what nineteenth-century employers believed: people need us more than we need them. But, in fact, organizations have to market membership as much as they market products and services—and perhaps more. They have to attract people, hold people, recognize and reward people, motivate people, and serve and satisfy people.

The relationship between knowledge workers and their organizations is a distinctly new phenomenon, one for which we have no good term. For example, an employee, by definition, is someone who gets paid for working. Yet the largest single group of "employees" in the United States is comprised of the millions of men and women who work several hours a week without pay for one or another nonprofit organization. They are clearly "staff" and consider themselves as such, but they are unpaid volunteers. Similarly, many people who work as employees are not employed in any legal sense because they do not work for someone else. Fifty or sixty years ago, we would have spoken of these people (many, if not most, of whom are educated professionals) as "independent"; today we speak of the "self-employed."

These discrepancies—and they exist in just about every language—remind us why new realities often demand new words. But until such a word emerges, this is probably the best definition of employees in the post-capitalist society: people whose ability to make a contribution depends on having access to an organization.

As far as the employees who work in subordinate and menial occupations are concerned–the sales-clerk in the supermarket, the cleaning woman in the hospital, the delivery-truck driver–the consequences of this new definition are small. For all practical purposes, their position may not be too different from that of the wage earner, the "worker" of yesterday, whose direct descendants they are. In fact, this is precisely one of the central social problems modern society faces.

But the relationship between the organization and knowledge workers, who already number at least one-third and more likely two-fifths of all employees, is radically different, as is that between the organization and volunteers. They can work only because there is an organization, thus they too are dependent. But at the same time, they own the "means of production"–their knowledge. In this respect, they are independent and highly mobile.

Knowledge workers still need the tools of production. In fact, capital investment in the tools of the knowledge employee may already be higher than the capital investment in the tools of the manufacturing worker ever was. (And the social investment, for example, the investment in a knowledge worker's education, is many times the investment in the manual worker's education.) But this capital investment is unproductive unless the knowledge worker brings to bear on it the knowledge that he or she owns and that cannot be taken away. Machine operators in the factory did as they were told. The machine decided not only what to do but how to do it. The knowledge employee may well need a machine, whether it be a computer, an ultrasound analyzer, or a telescope. But the machine will not tell the knowledge worker what to do, let alone how to do it. And without this knowledge, which belongs to the employee, the machine is unproductive.

Further, machine operators, like all workers throughout history, could be told what to do, how to do it, and how fast to do it. Knowledge workers cannot be supervised effectively. Unless they know more about their specialty than anybody else in the organization, they are basically useless. The marketing manager may tell the market researcher what the company needs to know about the design of a new product and the market segment in which it should be positioned. But it is the market researcher's job to tell the president of the company what market research is needed, how to set it up, and what the results mean.

During the traumatic restructuring of American business in the 1980s, thousands, if not hundreds of thousands, of knowledge employees lost their jobs. Their companies were acquired, merged, spun off, or liquidated. Yet within a few months, most of them found new jobs in which to put their knowledge to work. The transition period was painful, and in about half the cases, the new job did not pay quite as much as the old one did and may not have been as enjoyable. But the laid-off technicians, professionals, and managers found they had the "capital," the knowledge: they owned the means of production. Somebody else, the organization, had the tools of production. The two needed each other.

One consequence of this new relationship—and it is another new tension in modern society—is that loyalty can no longer be obtained by the paycheck. The organization must earn loyalty by proving to its knowledge employees that it offers them exceptional opportunities for putting their knowledge to work. Not so long ago we talked about "labor." Increasingly we are talking about "human resources." This change reminds us that it is the individual, and especially the skilled and knowledgeable employee, who decides in large measure what he or she will contribute to the organization and how great the yield from his or her knowledge will be.

B E C A U S E the modern organization consists of knowledge specialists, it has to be an organization of equals, of colleagues and associates. No knowledge ranks higher than another; each is judged by its contribution to the common task rather than by any inherent superiority or inferiority. Therefore, the modern organization cannot be an organization of boss and subordinate. It must be organized as a team.

There are only three kinds of teams. One is the sort of team that plays together in tennis doubles. In that team—and it has to be small—each member adapts himself or herself to the personality, the skills, the strengths, and the weaknesses of the other member or members. Then there is the team that plays European football or soccer. Each player has a fixed position; but the whole team moves together (except for the goalie) while individual members retain their relative positions. Finally, there is the American baseball team—or the orchestra—in which all the members have fixed positions.

At any given time, an organization can play only one kind of game. And it can use only one kind of team for any given task. Which team to use or game to play is one of the riskiest decisions in the life of an organization. Few things are as difficult in an organization as transforming from one kind of team to another.

Traditionally, American industry used a baseball-style team to produce a new product or model. Research did its work and passed it on to engineering. Engineering did its work and passed it on to manufacturing. Manufacturing did its work and passed it on to marketing. Accounting usually came in at the manufacturing phase. Personnel usually came in only when there was a true crisis—and often not even then.

Then the Japanese reorganized their new product development into a soccer team. In such a team, each function does its own work, but from the beginning they work together. They move with the task, so to speak, the way a soccer team moves with the ball. It took the Japanese at least 15 years to learn how to do this. But once they had mastered the new concept, they cut development time by two-thirds. Where traditionally it has taken five years to bring out a new automobile model, Toyota, Nissan, and Honda now do it in eighteen months. This, as much as their quality control, has given the Japanese the upper hand in both the American and European automobile markets.

Some American manufacturers have been working hard to reorganize their development work according to the Japanese model. Ford Motor Company, for instance, began to do so in the early 1980s. Ten years later, in the early 1990s, it has made considerable progress—but not nearly enough to catch up with the Japanese. Changing a team demands the most difficult learning imaginable: unlearning. It demands giving up hard-earned skills, habits of a lifetime, deeply cherished values of craftsmanship and professionalism, and—perhaps the most difficult of all—it demands giving up old and treasured human relationships. It means abandoning what people have always considered "our community" or "our family."

But if the organization is to perform, it must be organized as a team. When modern organizations first arose in the closing years of the nineteenth century, the only model was the military. The Prussian Army was as much a marvel of organization for the world of 1870 as Henry Ford's assembly line was for the world of 1920. In the army of 1870, each member did much the same thing, and the number of people with any knowledge was infinitesimally small. The army was organized by command-and-control, and business enterprise as well as most other institutions copied that model. This is now rapidly changing. As more and more organizations become information-based, they are transforming themselves into soccer or tennis teams, that is, into responsibility-based organizations in which every member must act as a responsible decision maker. All members, in other words, have to see themselves as "executives."

Even so, an organization must be managed. The management may be intermittent and perfunctory, as it is, for instance, in the Parent-Teacher Association at a U.S. suburban school. Or management may be a full-time and demanding job for a fairly large group of people, as it is in the military, the business enterprise, the labor union, and the university. But there have to be people who make decisions or nothing will ever get done. There have to be people who are accountable for the organization's mission, its spirit, its performance, its results. Society, community, and family may have "leaders," but only organizations know a "management." And while this management must have considerable authority, its job in the modern organization is not to command. It is to inspire.

THE society of organizations is unprecedented in human history. It is unprecedented in its performance capacity both because each of its constituent organizations is a highly specialized tool designed for one specific task and because each bases itself on the organization and deployment of knowledge. It is unprecedented in its structure. But it is also unprecedented in its tensions and problems. Not all of these are serious. In fact, some of them we already know how to resolve–issues of social responsibility, for example. But there are other areas where we do not know the right answer and where we may not even be asking the right questions yet.

There is, for instance, the tension between the community's need for continuity and stability and the organization's need to be an innovator and destabilizer. There is the split between "literati" and "managers." Both are needed: the former to produce knowledge, the latter to apply knowledge and make it productive. But the former focus on words and ideas, the latter on people, work, and performance. There is the threat to the very basis of the society of organizations–the knowledge base–that arises from ever greater specialization, from the shift from knowledge to *knowledges*. But the greatest and most difficult challenge is that presented by society's new pluralism.

For more than 600 years, no society has had as many centers of power as the society in which we now live. The Middle Ages indeed knew pluralism. Society was composed of hundreds of competing and autonomous power centers: feudal lords and knights, exempt bishoprics, autonomous monasteries, "free" cities. In some places, the Austrian Tyrol, for example, there were even "free peasants," beholden to no one but the Emperor. There were also autonomous craft guilds and transnational trading leagues like the Hanseatic Merchants and the merchant bankers of Florence, toll and tax collectors, local "parliaments" with legislative and tax-raising powers, private armies available for hire, and myriads more.

Modern history in Europe–and equally in Japan–has been the history of the subjugation of all competing centers of power by one central authority, first called the "prince," then the "state." By the middle of the nineteenth century, the unitary state had triumphed in every developed country except the United States, which remained profoundly pluralistic in its religious and educational organizations. Indeed, the abolition of pluralism was the "progressive" cause for nearly 600 years.

But just when the triumph of the state seemed assured, the first new organization arose–the large business enterprise. (This, of course, always happens when the "End of History" is announced.) Since then, one new organization after another has sprung up. And old organizations like the university, which in Europe seemed to have been brought safely under the control of central governments, have become autonomous again. Ironically, twentieth-century totalitarianism, especially communism, represented the last desperate attempt to save the old progressive creed in which there is only one center of power and one organization rather than a pluralism of competing and autonomous organizations.

That attempt failed, as we know. But the failure of central authority, in and of itself, does nothing to address the issues that follow from a pluralistic society. To illustrate, consider a story that many people have heard or, more accurately, misheard.

During his lifetime, Charles E. Wilson was a prominent personality in the United States, first as president and chief executive officer of General Motors, at that time the world's largest and most successful manufacturer, then as secretary of defense in the Eisenhower administration. But if Wilson is remembered at all today it is for something he did *not* say: "What is good for General Motors is good for the United States." What Wilson actually said in his 1953 confirmation hearings for the Defense Department job was: "What is good for the United States is good for General Motors."

Wilson tried for the remainder of his life to correct the misquote. But no one listened to him. Everyone argued, "If he didn't say it, he surely believes it—in fact he *should* believe it." For as has been said, executives in an organization—whether business or university or hospital or the Boy Scouts—must believe that its mission and task are society's most important mission and task as well as the foundation for everything else. If they do not believe this, their organization will soon lose faith in itself, self-confidence, pride, and the ability to perform.

The diversity that is characteristic of a developed society and that provides its great strength is only possible because of the specialized, single-task organizations that we have developed since the Industrial Revolution and, especially, during the last 50 years. But the feature that gives them the capacity to perform is precisely that each is autonomous and specialized, informed only by its own narrow mission and vision, its own narrow values, and not by any consideration of society and community.

Therefore, we come back to the old–and never resolved–problem of the pluralistic society: Who takes care of the Common Good? Who defines it? Who balances the separate and often competing goals and values of society's institutions? Who makes the trade-off decisions and on what basis should they be made?

Medieval feudalism was replaced by the unitary sovereign state precisely because it could not answer these questions. But the unitary sovereign state has now itself been replaced by a new pluralism–a pluralism of function rather than one of political power–because it could neither satisfy the needs of society nor perform the necessary tasks of community. That, in the final analysis, is the most fundamental lesson to be learned from the failure of socialism, the failure of the belief in the all-embracing and all-powerful state. The challenge that faces us now, and especially in the developed, free-market democracies such as the United States, is to make the pluralism of autonomous, knowledge-based organizations redound both to economic performance and to political and social cohesion.

10   What Business Can Learn from Nonprofits

T HE GIRL SCOUTS, the Red Cross, the pastoral churches—
our nonprofit organizations—are becoming America's management
leaders. In two areas, strategy and the effectiveness of the board,
they are practicing what most American businesses only preach.
And in the most crucial area—the motivation and productivity of
knowledge workers—they are truly pioneers, working out the policies and practices that business will have to learn tomorrow.

Few people are aware that the nonprofit sector is by far America's
largest employer. Every other adult—a total of 80 million plus people—
works as a volunteer, giving on average nearly five hours each week
to one or several nonprofit organizations. This is equal to 10 million
full-time jobs. Were volunteers paid, their wages, even at minimum
rate, would amount to some $150 billion, or 5 percent of GNP. And
volunteer work is changing fast. To be sure, what many do requires
little skill or judgment: collecting in the neighborhood for the Community Chest one Saturday afternoon a year, chaperoning youngsters selling Girl Scout cookies door to door, driving old people to
the doctor. But more and more volunteers are becoming "unpaid
staff," taking over the professional and managerial tasks in their
organizations.

Not all nonprofits have been doing well, of course. A good many
community hospitals are in dire straits. Traditional churches and
synagogues of all persuasions—liberal, conservative, evangelical,

July–August 1989

fundamentalist–are still steadily losing members. Indeed, the sector overall has not expanded in the last 10 or 15 years, either in terms of the money it raises (when adjusted for inflation) or in the number of volunteers. Yet in its productivity, in the scope of its work and in its contribution to American society, the nonprofit sector has grown tremendously in the last two decades.

The Salvation Army is an example. People convicted to their first prison term in Florida, mostly very poor black or Hispanic youths, are now paroled into the Salvation Army's custody–about 25,000 each year. Statistics show that if these young men and women go to jail the majority will become habitual criminals. But the Salvation Army has been able to rehabilitate 80 percent of them through a strict work program run largely by volunteers. And the program costs a fraction of what it would to keep the offenders behind bars.

Underlying this program and many other effective nonprofit endeavors is a commitment to management. Twenty years ago, management was a dirty word for those involved in nonprofit organizations. It meant business, and nonprofits prided themselves on being free of the taint of commercialism and above such sordid considerations as the bottom line. Now most of them have learned that nonprofits need management even more than business does, precisely because they lack the discipline of the bottom line. The nonprofits are, of course, still dedicated to "doing good." But they also realize that good intentions are no substitute for organization and leadership, for accountability, performance, and results. Those require management and that, in turn, begins with the organization's mission.

As a rule, nonprofits are more money-conscious than business enterprises are. They talk and worry about money much of the time because it is so hard to raise and because they always have so much less of it than they need. But nonprofits do not base their strategy on money, nor do they make it the center of their plans, as so many corporate executives do. "The businesses I work with start their planning with financial returns," says one well-known CEO who sits on both business and nonprofit boards. "The nonprofits start with the performance of their mission."

Starting with the mission and its requirements may be the first lesson business can learn from successful nonprofits. It focuses the organization on action. It defines the specific strategies needed to attain the crucial goals. It creates a disciplined organization. It alone can prevent the most common degenerative disease of organizations, especially large ones: splintering their always limited resources on things that are "interesting" or look "profitable" rather than concentrating them on a very small number of productive efforts.

The best nonprofits devote a great deal of thought to defining their organization's mission. They avoid sweeping statements full of good intentions and focus, instead, on objectives that have clear-cut implications for the work their members perform—staff and volunteers both. The Salvation Army's goal, for example, is to turn society's rejects—alcoholics, criminals, derelicts—into citizens. The Girl Scouts help youngsters become confident, capable young women who respect themselves and other people. The Nature Conservancy preserves the diversity of nature's fauna and flora. Nonprofits also start with the environment, the community, the "customers" to be; they do not, as American businesses tend to do, start with the inside, that is, with the organization or with financial returns.

Willowcreek Community Church in South Barrington, Illinois, outside Chicago, has become the nation's largest church—some 13,000 parishioners. Yet it is barely 15 years old. Bill Hybels, in his early twenties when he founded the church, chose the community because it had relatively few churchgoers, though the population was growing fast and churches were plentiful. He went from door to door asking, "Why don't you go to church?" Then he designed a church to answer the potential customers' needs: for instance, it offers full services on Wednesday evenings because many working parents need Sunday to spend with their children. Moreover, Hybels continues to listen and react. The pastor's sermon is taped while it is being delivered and instantly reproduced so that parishioners can pick up a cassette when they leave the building because he was told again and again, "I need to listen when I drive home or drive to work so that I can build the message into my life." But he was also told: "The sermon always tells me to change my life but never how to do it." So now every one of Hybels's sermons ends with specific action recommendations.

A well-defined mission serves as a constant reminder of the need to look outside the organization not only for "customers" but also for measures of success. The temptation to content oneself with the "goodness of our cause"–and thus to substitute good intentions for results–always exists in nonprofit organizations. It is precisely because of this that the successful and performing nonprofits have learned to define clearly what changes *outside* the organization constitute "results" and to focus on them.

The experience of one large Catholic hospital chain in the Southwest shows how productive a clear sense of mission and a focus on results can be. Despite the sharp cuts in Medicare payments and hospital stays during the past eight years, this chain has increased revenues by 15 percent (thereby managing to break even) while greatly expanding its services and raising both patient-care and medical standards. It has done so because the nun who is its CEO understood that she and her staff are in the business of delivering health care (especially to the poor), not running hospitals.

As a result, when health care delivery began moving out of hospitals for medical rather than economic reasons about ten years ago, the chain promoted the trend instead of fighting it. It founded ambulatory surgery centers, rehabilitation centers, X-ray and lab networks, HMOs, and so on. The chain's motto was: "If it's in the patient's interest, we have to promote it; it's then our job to make it pay." Paradoxically, the policy has filled the chain's hospitals; the freestanding facilities are so popular they generate a steady stream of referrals.

This is, of course, not so different from the marketing strategy of successful Japanese companies. But it is very different indeed from the way most Western businesses think and operate. And the difference is that the Catholic nuns–and the Japanese–start with the mission rather than with their own rewards, and with what they have to make happen outside themselves, in the marketplace, to deserve a reward.

Finally, a clearly defined mission will foster innovative ideas and help others understand why they need to be implemented–however much they fly in the face of tradition. To illustrate, consider the Daisy Scouts, a program for five-year-olds which the Girl Scouts initiated a few years back. For 75 years, first grade had been the minimum age for entry into a Brownie troop, and many Girl Scout councils wanted to keep it that way. Others, however, looked at demographics and saw the growing numbers of working women with "latch key" kids. They also looked at the children and realized that they were far more sophisticated than their predecessors a generation ago (largely thanks to TV).

Today the Daisy Scouts are 100,000 strong and growing fast. It is by far the most successful of the many programs for preschoolers that have been started these last 20 years, and far more successful than any of the very expensive government programs. Moreover, it is so far the only program that has seen these critical demographic changes and children's exposure to long hours of TV viewing as an opportunity.

M<small>ANY</small> nonprofits now have what is still the exception in business—a functioning board. They also have something even rarer: a CEO who is clearly accountable to the board and whose performance is reviewed annually by a board committee. And they have what is rarer still: a board whose performance is reviewed annually against preset performance objectives. Effective use of the board is thus a second area in which business can learn from the nonprofit sector.

In U.S. law, the board of directors is still considered the "managing" organ of the corporation. Management authors and scholars agree that strong boards are essential and have been writing to that effect for more than 20 years, beginning with Myles Mace's pioneering work.[1] Nevertheless, the top managements of our large companies have been whittling away at the directors' role, power, and independence for more than half a century. In every single business failure of a large company in the last few decades, the board was the last to realize that things were going wrong. To find a truly effective board, you are much better advised to look in the nonprofit sector than in our public corporations.

In part, this difference is a product of history. Traditionally, the board has run the shop in nonprofit organizations—or tried to. In fact, it is only because nonprofits have grown too big and complex to be run by part-time outsiders, meeting for three hours a month, that so many have shifted to professional management. The American Red Cross is probably the largest nongovernmental agency in the world and certainly one of the most complex. It is responsible for worldwide disaster relief; it runs thousands of blood banks as well as the bone and skin banks in hospitals; it conducts training in cardiac and respiratory rescue nationwide; and it gives first-aid courses in thousands of schools. Yet it did not have a paid chief executive until 1950, and its first professional CEO came only with the Reagan era.

But however common professional management becomes–and professional CEOs are now found in most nonprofits and all the bigger ones–nonprofit boards cannot, as a rule, be rendered impotent the way so many business boards have been. No matter how much nonprofit CEOs would welcome it–and quite a few surely would–nonprofit boards cannot become their rubber stamp. Money is one reason. Few directors in publicly held corporations are substantial shareholders, whereas directors on nonprofit boards very often contribute large sums themselves, and are expected to bring in donors as well. But also, nonprofit directors tend to have a personal commitment to the organization's cause. Few people sit on a church vestry or on a school board unless they deeply care about religion or education. Moreover, nonprofit board members typically have served as volunteers themselves for a good many years and are deeply knowledgeable about the organization, unlike outside directors in a business.

Precisely because the nonprofit board is so committed and active, its relationship with the CEO tends to be highly contentious and full of potential for friction. Nonprofit CEOs complain that their board "meddles." The directors, in turn, complain that management "usurps" the board's function. This has forced an increasing number of nonprofits to realize that neither board nor CEO is "the boss." They are colleagues, working for the same goal but each having a different task. And they have learned that it is the CEO's responsibility to define the tasks of each, the board's and his or her own.

For example, a large electric co-op in the Pacific Northwest created ten board committees, one for every member. Each has a specific work assignment: community relations, electricity rates, personnel, service standards, and so on. Together with the co-op's volunteer chairman and its paid CEO, each of these one-person committees defines its one-year and three-year objectives and the work needed to attain them, which usually requires five to eight days a year from the board member. The chairman reviews each member's work and performance every year, and a member whose performance is found wanting two years in a row cannot stand for reelection. In addition, the chairman, together with three other board members, annually reviews the performance of the entire board and of the CEO.

The key to making a board effective, as this example suggests, is not to talk about its function but to organize its work. More and more nonprofits are doing just that, among them half a dozen fair-sized liberal arts colleges, a leading theological seminary, and some large research hospitals and museums. Ironically, these approaches reinvent the way the first nonprofit board in America was set up 300 years ago: the Harvard University Board of Overseers. Each member is assigned as a "visitor" to one area in the university–the Medical School, the Astronomy Department, the investment of the endowment–and acts both as a source of knowledge to that area and as a critic of its performance. It is a common saying in American academia that Harvard has the only board that makes a difference.

The weakening of the large corporation's board would, many of us predicted (beginning with Myles Mace), weaken management rather than strengthen it. It would diffuse management's account-ability for performance and results; and indeed, it is the rare big-company board that reviews the CEO's performance against preset business objectives. Weakening the board would also, we predicted, deprive top management of effective and credible support if it were attacked. These predictions have been borne out amply in the recent rash of hostile takeovers.

To restore management's ability to manage we will have to make boards effective again–and that should be considered a responsibil-ity of the CEO. A few first steps have been taken. The audit committee in most companies now has a real rather than a make-believe job responsibility. A few companies–though so far almost no large ones–have a small board committee on succession and executive develop-ment, which regularly meets with senior executives to discuss their performance and their plans. But I know of no company so far where there are work plans for the board and any kind of review of the board's performance. And few do what the larger nonprofits now do routinely: put a new board member through systematic training.

NONPROFITS used to say, "We don't pay volunteers so we cannot make demands upon them." Now they are more likely to say, "Volunteers must get far greater satisfaction from their accomplishments and make a greater contribution precisely because they do not get a paycheck." The steady transformation of the volunteer from well-meaning amateur to trained, professional, unpaid staff member is the most significant development in the nonprofit sector–as well as the one with the most far-reaching implications for tomorrow's businesses.

A Midwestern Catholic diocese may have come furthest in this process. It now has fewer than half the priests and nuns it had only 15 years ago. Yet it has greatly expanded its activities–in some cases, such as help for the homeless and for drug abusers, more than doubling them. It still has many traditional volunteers like the Altar Guild members who arrange flowers. But now it is also being served by some 2,000 part-time unpaid staff who run the Catholic charities, perform administrative jobs in parochial schools, and organize youth activities, college Newman Clubs, and even some retreats.

A similar change has taken place at the First Baptist Church in Richmond, Virginia, one of the largest and oldest churches in the Southern Baptist Convention. When Dr. Peter James Flamming took over five years ago, the church had been going downhill for many years, as is typical of old, inner-city churches. Today it again has 4,000 communicants and runs a dozen community outreach programs as well as a full complement of in-church ministries. The church has only nine paid full-time employees. But of its 4,000 communicants, 1,000 serve as unpaid staff.

This development is by no means confined to religious organizations. The American Heart Association has chapters in every city of any size throughout the country. Yet its paid staff is limited to those at national headquarters, with just a few traveling troubleshooters serving the field. Volunteers manage and staff the chapters, with full responsibility for community health education as well as fund raising.

These changes are, in part, a response to need. With close to half the adult population already serving as volunteers, their overall number is unlikely to grow. And with money always in short supply, the nonprofits cannot add paid staff. If they want to add to their activities–and needs are growing–they have to make volunteers more productive, have to give them more work and more responsibility. But the major impetus for the change in the volunteer's role has come from the volunteers themselves.

More and more volunteers are educated people in managerial or professional jobs–some preretirement men and women in their fifties, even more baby-boomers who are reaching their mid-thirties or forties. These people are not satisfied with being helpers. They are knowledge workers in the jobs in which they earn their living, and they want to be knowledge workers in the jobs in which they contribute to society–that is, their volunteer work. If nonprofit organizations want to attract and hold them, they have to put their competence and knowledge to work. They have to offer meaningful achievement.

Many nonprofits systematically recruit for such people. Seasoned volunteers are assigned to scan the newcomers–the new member in a church or synagogue, the neighbor who collects for the Red Cross to find those with leadership talent and persuade them to try themselves in more demanding assignments. Then senior staff (either a full-timer on the payroll or a seasoned volunteer) interviews the newcomers to assess their strengths and place them accordingly. Volunteers may also be assigned both a mentor and a supervisor with whom they work out their performance goals. These advisers are two different people, as a rule, and both, ordinarily, volunteers themselves.

The Girl Scouts, which employs 730,000 volunteers and only 6,000 paid staff for 3.5 million girl members, works this way. A volunteer typically starts by driving youngsters once a week to a meeting. Then a more seasoned volunteer draws her into other work–accompanying Girl Scouts selling cookies door-to-door, assisting a Brownie leader on a camping trip. Out of this step-by-step process evolve the volunteer boards of the local councils and, eventually, the Girl Scouts governing organ, the National Board. Each step, even the very first, has its own compulsory training program, usually conducted by a woman who is herself a volunteer. Each has specific performance standards and performance goals.

What do these unpaid staff people themselves demand? What makes them stay—and, of course, they can leave at any time. Their first and most important demand is that the nonprofit have a clear mission, one that drives everything the organization does. A senior vice president in a large regional bank has two small children. Yet she just took over as chair of the state chapter of Nature Conservancy, which finds, buys, and manages endangered natural ecologies. "I love my job," she said, when I asked her why she took on such heavy additional work, "and of course the bank has a creed. But it doesn't really know what it contributes. At Nature Conservancy, I know what I am here for."

The second thing this new breed requires, indeed demands, is training, training, and more training. And, in turn, the most effective way to motivate and hold veterans is to recognize their expertise and use them to train newcomers. Then these knowledge workers demand responsibility—above all, for thinking through and setting their own performance goals. They expect to be consulted and to participate in making decisions that affect their work and the work of the organization as a whole. And they expect opportunities for advancement, that is, a chance to take on more demanding assignments and more responsibility as their performance warrants. That is why a good many nonprofits have developed career ladders for their volunteers.

Supporting all this activity is accountability. Many of today's knowledge-worker volunteers insist on having their performance reviewed against preset objectives at least once a year. And increasingly, they expect their organizations to remove nonperformers by moving them to other assignments that better fit their capacities or by counseling them to leave. "It's worse than the Marine Corps boot camp," says the priest in charge of volunteers in the Midwestern diocese, "but we have 400 people on the waiting list." One large and growing Midwestern art museum requires of its volunteers—board members, fundraisers, docents, and the people who edit the museum's newsletter—that they set their goals each year, appraise themselves against these goals each year, and resign when they fail to meet their goals two years in a row. So does a fair-sized Jewish organization working on college campuses.

These volunteer professionals are still a minority, but a significant one—perhaps a tenth of the total volunteer population. And they are growing in numbers and, more important, in their impact on the nonprofit sector. Increasingly, nonprofits say what the minister in a large pastoral church says: "There is no laity in this church; there are only pastors, a few paid, most unpaid."

T HIS MOVE from nonprofit volunteer to unpaid professional may be the most important development in American society today. We hear a great deal about the decay and dissolution of family and community and about the loss of values. And, of course, there is reason for concern. But the nonprofits are generating a powerful countercurrent. They are forging new bonds of community, a new commitment to active citizenship, to social responsibility, to values. And surely what the nonprofit contributes to the volunteer is as important as what the volunteer contributes to the nonprofit. Indeed, it may be fully as important as the service, whether religious, educational, or welfare related, that the nonprofit provides in the community.

This development also carries a clear lesson for business. Managing the knowledge worker for productivity is the challenge ahead for American management. The nonprofits are showing us how to do that. It requires a clear mission, careful placement and continuous learning and teaching, management by objectives and self-control, high demands but corresponding responsibility, and accountability for performance and results.

There is also, however, a clear warning to American business in this transformation of volunteer work. The students in the program for senior and middle-level executives in which I teach work in a wide diversity of businesses: banks and insurance companies, large retail chains, aerospace and computer companies, real estate developers, and many others. But most of them also serve as volunteers in nonprofits—in a church, on the board of the college they graduated from, as scout leaders, with the YMCA or the Community Chest or the local symphony orchestra. When I ask them why they do it, far too many give the same answer: Because in my job there isn't much challenge, not enough achievement, not enough responsibility; and there is no mission, there is only expediency.

11 The New Productivity Challenge

T HE SINGLE greatest challenge facing managers in the developed countries of the world is to raise the productivity of knowledge and service workers. This challenge, which will dominate the management agenda for the next several decades, will ultimately determine the competitive performance of companies. Even more important, it will determine the very fabric of society and the quality of life in every industrialized nation.

For the last 120 years, productivity in making and moving things—in manufacturing, farming, mining, construction, and transportation—has risen in developed countries at an annual rate of 3 percent to 4 percent, a 45-fold expansion overall. On this explosive growth rest all the gains these nations and their citizens have enjoyed: vast increases in disposable income and purchasing power; ever-wider access to education and health care; and the availability of leisure time, something known only to aristocrats and the "idle rich" before 1914, when everyone else worked at least 3,000 hours a year. (Today even the Japanese work no more than about 2,000 hours each year, while Americans average 1,800 hours and West Germans 1,650.)

Now these gains are unraveling, but not because productivity in making and moving things has fallen. Contrary to popular belief,

November–December 1991

productivity in these activities is still going up at much the same rate. And it is rising fully as much in the United States as it is in Japan or West Germany. Indeed, the increase in U.S. manufacturing productivity during the 1980s–some 3.9 percent a year–was actually larger in absolute terms than the corresponding annual increases in Japan and Germany, while the 4 percent to 5 percent annual rise in U.S. agricultural productivity is far and away the largest recorded anywhere at any time.

The productivity revolution is over because there are too few people employed in making and moving things for their productivity to be decisive. All told, they account for no more than one-fifth of the workforce in developed economies. Only 30 years ago, they were still a near-majority. Even Japan, which is still manufacturing intensive, can no longer expect increased productivity in that sector to sustain its economic growth. Indeed, the great majority of working people in Japan are knowledge and service workers with productivities as low as those in any other developed country. And when farmers make up only 3 percent of the employed population, as they do in the United States, Japan, and most of Western Europe, even record increases in their output add virtually nothing to their country's overall productivity and wealth.

The chief *economic* priority for developed countries, therefore, must be to raise the productivity of knowledge and service work. The country that does this first will dominate the twenty-first century economically. The most pressing *social* challenge developed countries face, however, will be to raise the productivity of service work. Unless this challenge is met, the developed world will face increasing social tensions, increasing polarization, increasing radicalization, possibly even class war.

In developed economies, opportunities for careers and promotion are more and more limited to people with advanced schooling, people qualified for knowledge work. But these men and women will always be a minority. They will always be outnumbered by people who lack the qualifications for anything but low-skilled service jobs–people who in their social position are comparable to the "proletarians" of 100 years ago, the poorly educated, unskilled masses who thronged the exploding industrial cities and streamed into their factories.

In the early 1880s, intelligent observers of every political persuasion were obsessed with the specter of class war between the industrial proletariat and the bourgeoisie. Karl Marx was hardly alone in predicting that the "immiserization" of the proletariat would lead inevitably to revolution. Benjamin Disraeli, perhaps the greatest of the nineteenth century conservatives, was equally persuaded of the inevitability of class war. And Henry James, the chronicler of American wealth and European aristocracy, was so frightened by the prospect that he made it the central theme of *The Princess Casamassima*, one of his most haunting novels.

What defeated these prophecies, which seemed eminently reasonable, indeed almost self-evident to contemporaries, was the revolution in productivity set off by Frederick W. Taylor in 1881, when he began to study the way a common laborer shoveled sand. Taylor himself worked in an iron foundry and was deeply shocked by the bitter animosity between the workers and managers. Fearful that this hatred would ultimately lead to class war, he set out to improve the efficiency of industrial work. And his efforts, in turn, sparked the revolution that allowed industrial workers to earn middle-class wages and achieve middle-class status despite their lack of skill and education. By 1930, when according to Marx the revolution of the proletariat should have been a fait accompli, the proletariat had become the bourgeoisie.

Now it is time for another productivity revolution. This time, however, history is on our side. In the past century, we have learned a great deal about productivity and how to raise it—enough to know that we need a revolution, enough to know how to start one.

KNOWLEDGE and service workers range from research scientists and cardiac surgeons through draftswomen and store managers to 16-year-olds who flip hamburgers in fast-food restaurants on Saturday afternoons. Their ranks also include people whose work makes them "machine operators": dishwashers, janitors, data-entry operators. Yet for all their diversity in knowledge, skill, responsibility, social status, and pay, knowledge and service workers are remarkably alike in two crucial respects: what does not work in raising their productivity and what does.

The first thing we have learned—and it came as a rude shock—is about what does not work. Capital cannot be substituted for labor. Nor will new technology by itself generate higher productivity. In making and moving things, capital and technology are *factors* of production, to use the economist's term. In knowledge and service work, they are *tools* of production. The difference is that a factor can replace labor, while a tool may or may not. Whether tools help productivity or harm it depends on what people do with them, on the purpose to which they are being put, for instance, or on the skill of the user. Thirty years ago, for example, we were sure the efficiency of the computer would lead to massive reductions in clerical and office staff. The promise of greater productivity led to massive investments in data-processing equipment that now rival those in materials-processing technology (that is, in conventional machinery). Yet office and clerical forces have grown at a much faster rate since the introduction of information technology than ever before. And there has been virtually no increase in the productivity of service work.

Hospitals are a telling example. In the late 1940s, they were entirely labor intensive, with little capital investment except in bricks, mortar, and beds. A good many perfectly respectable hospitals had not even invested in readily available, fairly old technologies: they provided neither x-ray departments nor clinical laboratories nor physical therapy. Today hospitals are hugely capital intensive, with enormous sums invested in ultrasound, body scanners, nuclear magnetic imagers, blood and tissue analyzers, clean rooms, and a dozen more new technologies. Each piece of equipment has brought with it the need for more highly paid people but has not reduced the existing staff by a single person. (In fact, the worldwide escalation of health-care costs is largely the result of the hospital's having become a labor-intensive and capital-intensive monstrosity.) But hospitals, at least, have significantly increased their performance capacity. In other areas of knowledge or service work there are only higher costs, more investment, and more people.

Massive increases in productivity are the only way out of this morass. And these increases can only come from what Taylor called "working smarter."[1] Simply, this means working more productively without working harder or longer.

The economist sees capital investment as the key to productivity;

the technologist gives star billing to new machines. Nevertheless, the main force behind the productivity explosion has been working smarter. Capital investment and technology were as copious in the developed economies during the first 100 years of the Industrial Revolution as they have been in its second 100 years. It was only with the advent of working smarter that productivity in making and moving things took off on its meteoric rise.

And so it will be for knowledge and service work–with this difference: in manufacturing, working smarter is only one key to increased productivity. In knowledge and service work, working smarter is the only key. What is more, it is a more complex key, one that requires looking closely at work in ways that Taylor never dreamed of.

When Taylor studied the shoveling of sand, the only question that concerned him was, "How is it done?" Almost 50 years later, when Harvard's Elton Mayo set out to demolish Taylor's "scientific management" and replace it with what later came to be called "human relations," he focused on the same question. In his experiments at Western Electric's Hawthorne Works, Mayo asked, "How can wiring telephone equipment best be done?" The point is that in making and moving things, the task is always taken for granted.

In knowledge and service work, however, the first questions in increasing productivity–and working smarter–have to be, "What is the task? What are we trying to accomplish? Why do it at all?" The easiest, but perhaps also the greatest, productivity gains in such work will come from defining the task and especially from eliminating what does not need to be done.[2]

A very old example is still one of the best: mail-order processing at the early Sears, Roebuck. Between 1906 and 1908, Sears eliminated the time-consuming job of counting the money in incoming mail orders. Rather than open the money envelopes enclosed with the orders, Sears weighed them automatically. In those days, virtually all Sears customers paid with coins. If the weight of the envelope tallied with the amount of the order within fairly narrow limits, the envelope went unopened. Similarly, Sears eliminated the even more time-consuming task of recording each incoming order by scheduling order handling and shipping according to the weight of the incoming mail (assuming 40 orders for each pound of mail). Within two years, these steps accounted for a tenfold increase in the productivity of the entire mail-order operation.[5]

A major insurance company recently increased the productivity of its claims-settlement department nearly fivefold—from an average of fifteen minutes per claim to three minutes—by eliminating detailed checking on all but very large claims. Instead of verifying 30 items as they had always done, the adjusters now check only four: whether the policy is still in force; whether the face amount matches the amount of the claim; whether the name of the policyholder matches the name on the death certificate; and whether the name of the beneficiary matches the name of the claimant. What provoked the change was asking, "What is the task?" and then answering, "To pay death claims as fast and as cheaply as possible." All that the company now requires to control the process is to work through a 2 percent sample, that is, every fiftieth claim, the traditional way.

Similarly, a few hospitals have taken most of the labor and expense out of their admissions process by admitting all patients the way they used to admit emergency cases who were brought in unconscious or bleeding and unable to fill out lengthy forms. These hospitals asked, "What is the task?" and answered, "To identify the patient's name, sex, age, address and how to bill"—information found on the insurance identification cards practically all patients carry.

These are both examples of service work. In knowledge work, defining the task and getting rid of what does not need to be done is even more necessary and produces even greater results. Consider how one multinational company redefined its strategic planning.

For many years, a planning staff of 45 brilliant people carefully prepared strategic scenarios in minute detail. The documents were first-class works and made stimulating reading, everybody agreed. But they had a minimal impact on operations. Then a new CEO asked, "What is the task?" and answered, "To give our businesses direction and goals and the strategy to attain these goals." It took four years of hard work and several false starts. But now the planning people (still about the same number) work through only three questions for each of the company's businesses: What market standing does it need to maintain leadership? What innovative performance does it need to support that standing? And what is the minimum rate of return needed to earn the cost of capital? Then the planning people work with the operating executives in each business to map out broad strategic guidelines for achieving these goals under various economic conditions. The results are far simpler and much less elegant, but they have become the "flight plans" that guide the company's businesses and its senior executives.

W̲H̲E̲N̲ people make or move things, they do one task at a time. Taylor's laborer shoveled sand; he did not also stoke the furnace. Mayo's wiring-room women soldered; they did not test finished telephones on the side. The Iowa farmer planting corn does not get off his tractor between rows to attend a meeting. Knowledge and service work, too, require concentration. The surgeon does not take telephone calls in the operating room, nor does the lawyer in consultation with a client.

But in organizations, where most knowledge and service work takes place, splintered attention is more and more the norm. The people at the very top can sometimes concentrate themselves (though far too few even try). But the great majority of engineers, teachers, salespeople, nurses, middle managers, and the like must carry a steadily growing load of busywork, activities that contribute little if any value and that have little if anything to do with what these professionals are qualified and paid for.

The worst case may be that of nurses in U.S. hospitals. We hear a great deal about the shortage of nurses. But how could it possibly be true? The number of graduates entering the profession has gone up steadily for a good many years. At the same time, the number of bed patients has been dropping sharply. The explanation of the paradox: nurses now spend only half their time doing what they have learned and are paid to do—nursing. The other half is eaten up by activities that do not require their skill and knowledge, add neither health-care nor economic value, and have little or nothing to do with patient care and patient well-being. Nurses are preoccupied, of course, with the avalanche of paperwork for Medicare, Medicaid, insurers, the billing office, and the prevention of malpractice suits.

The situation in higher education is not too different. Faculty in colleges and universities spend more and more hours in committee meetings instead of teaching in the classroom, advising students, or doing research. But few of these committees would ever be missed. And they would do a better job in less time if they had three instead of seven members.

Salespeople are just as splintered. In department stores, they now spend so much time serving computers that they have little time for serving customers–the main reason, perhaps, for the steady decline in their productivity as producers of sales and revenues. Field-sales representatives spend up to one-third of their time filling out reports rather than calling on customers. And engineers sit through meeting after meeting when they should be busy at their workstations.

This is not job enrichment; it is job impoverishment. It destroys productivity. It saps motivation and morale. Nurses, every attitude survey shows, bitterly resent not being able to spend more time caring for patients. They also believe, understandably, that they are grossly underpaid for what they are capable of doing, while the hospital administrator, equally understandably, believes that they are grossly overpaid for the unskilled clerical work they are actually doing.

The cure is fairly easy, as a rule. It is to concentrate the work–in this case, nursing–on the task–caring for patients. This is the second step toward working smarter. A few hospitals, for example, have taken the paperwork out of the nurse's job and given it to a floor clerk who also answers telephone calls from relatives and friends and arranges the flowers they send in. The level of patient care and the hours nurses devote to it have risen sharply. Yet the hospitals have also been able to reduce their nursing staffs by one-quarter or one-third and so raise salaries without incurring a higher nursing payroll.

To make these kinds of improvements, we must ask a second set of questions about every knowledge and service job: "What do we pay for? What value is this job supposed to add?" The answer is not always obvious or noncontroversial. One department store looked at its sales force and answered "sales," while another in the same metropolitan area and with much the same clientele answered "customer service." Each answer led to a different restructuring of the jobs on the sales floor. But each store achieved, and fairly fast, substantial growth in the revenues each salesperson and each department generated, that is, gains in both productivity and profitability.

For all its tremendous impact, Taylor's scientific management has had a bad press, especially in academia. Perhaps the main reason is the unrelenting campaign U.S. labor unions waged against it–and against Taylor himself–in the early years of this century. The unions did not oppose Taylor because they thought him antilabor or promanagement. He was neither. His unforgivable sin was his assertion that there is no such thing as "skill" in making and moving things. All such work was the same, Taylor asserted. And all could be analyzed step by step, as a series of unskilled operations that could then be combined into any kind of job. Anyone willing to learn these operations would be a "first-class man," deserving "first-class pay." He could do the most advanced work and do it to perfection.

To the skill-based unions of 1900, this assertion represented a direct attack. And this was especially true for the highly respected, extremely powerful unions that dominated what were then some of the country's most sophisticated manufacturing sites–the army arsenals and navy shipyards where nearly all peacetime production for the military took place until well after World World I. For these unions, each craft was a mystery whose secrets no member could divulge. Their power base was control of an apprenticeship that lasted five or seven years and admitted, as a rule, only relatives of members. And their workers were paid extremely well–more than most physicians of the day and triple what Taylor's first-class man could expect to get. No wonder that Taylor's assertions infuriated these aristocrats of labor.

Belief in the mystery of craft and skill persisted, as did the assumption that long years of apprenticeship were needed to acquire both. Indeed, Hitler went to war with the United States on the strength of that assumption. Convinced that it took five years or more to train optical craftsmen (whose skills are essential to modern warfare), he thought it would be at least that long before America could field an effective army and air force in Europe–and so declared war after the Japanese attack on Pearl Harbor.

We know now Taylor was right. The United States had almost no optical craftsmen in 1941. And modern warfare indeed requires precision optics in large quantities. But by applying Taylor's methods of scientific management, within a few months the United States trained semiskilled workers to turn out more highly advanced optics than even the Germans were producing, and on an assembly line to boot. And by that time, Taylor's first-class men with their increased productivity were also making a great deal more money than any craftsman of 1911 had ever dreamed of.

Eventually, knowledge work and service work may turn out to be like the work of making and moving things—that is, "just work," to use an old scientific management slogan. (At least this is what Taylor's true heirs, the more radical proponents of artificial intelligence, maintain.) But for the time being, we must not treat knowledge and service jobs as "just work." Nor can we assume they are homogeneous. Rather, these jobs can be divided into three distinct categories by looking at what productive performance in a given job actually represents. This process—defining performance—is the third step toward working smarter.

For some knowledge and service jobs, performance means quality. Take scientists in a research lab where quantity—the number of results—is quite secondary to their quality. One new drug that can generate annual sales of $500 million and dominate the market for a decade is infinitely more valuable than 20 "me too" drugs with annual sales of $20 million or $30 million each. The same principle applies to basic policy or strategic decisions, as well as to much less grandiose work, the physician's diagnosis, for example, or packaging design, or editing a magazine. In each of these instances, we do not yet know how to analyze the process that produces quality results. To raise productivity, therefore, we can only ask, "What works?"

The second category includes the majority of knowledge and service work: jobs in which quality and quantity together constitute performance. Department store sales are one example. Producing a "satisfied customer" is just as important as the dollar amount on the sales slip, but it is not so easy to define. Likewise, the quality of an architectural draftswoman's work is an integral part of her performance. But so is the number of drawings she can produce. The same holds true for engineers, sales reps in brokerage offices, medical technologists, branch bank managers, reporters, nurses, claims adjusters, and so on. Raising productivity in these jobs requires asking, "What works?" but also analyzing the process step by step and operation by operation.

Finally, there are a good many service jobs (filing, handling death claims, making hospital beds) in which performance is defined much as it is in making and moving things: that is, largely by quantity (for example, the number of minutes it takes to make up a hospital bed properly). In these "production" jobs, quality is primarily a matter of external criteria rather than an attribute of performance itself. Defining standards and building them into the work process is essential. But once this has been done, real productivity improvements will come through conventional industrial engineering, that is, through analyzing the task and combining the individual simple operations into a complete job.

D E F I N I N G the task, concentrating work on the task, and defining performance: by themselves, these three steps will produce substantial growth in productivity–perhaps most of what can be attained at any one time. They will need to be worked through again and again, maybe as often as every three or five years and certainly whenever work or its organization changes. But then, according to all the experience we have, the resulting productivity increases will equal, if not exceed, whatever industrial engineering, scientific management, or human relations ever achieved in manufacturing. In other words, they should give us the productivity revolution we need in knowledge and service work.

But on one condition only: that we apply what we have learned since World War II about increasing productivity in making and moving things. The fourth step toward working smarter, then, is for management to form a partnership with the people who hold the jobs, the people who are to become more productive. The goal has to be to build responsibility for productivity and performance into every knowledge and service job regardless of level, difficulty, or skill.

Frederick Taylor has often been criticized for never once asking the workers he studied how they thought their jobs could be improved. He told them. Nor did Elton Mayo ever ask; he also told. But Taylor's (and Mayo's, 40 years later) methodology was simply a product of the times, when the wisdom of the expert prevailed. (Freud, after all, never asked his patients what they thought their problems might be. Nor do we have any record that either Marx or Lenin ever thought of asking the masses.) Taylor considered both workers and managers "dumb oxen." And while Mayo had great respect for managers, he thought workers were "immature" and "maladjusted," deeply in need of the psychologist's expert guidance.

When World War II came, however, we had to ask the workers. We had no choice. U.S. factories had no engineers, psychologists, or foremen. They were all in uniform. To our immense surprise, as I still recollect, we discovered that the workers were neither dumb oxen nor immature nor maladjusted. They knew a great deal about the work they were doing—about its logic and rhythm, its quality, and its tools. Asking them what they thought was the way to address both productivity and quality.[4]

At first, only a few businesses accepted this novel proposition. (IBM was a pioneer and for a long time one of the few large companies to act on this idea.) But in the late 1950s and early 1960s, it was picked up by Japanese industrialists whose earlier attempts to return to prewar autocracy had collapsed in bloody strikes and near-civil war. Now, while still far from being widely practiced, it is at least generally accepted in theory that the workers' knowledge of their job is the starting point for improving productivity, quality, and performance.

In making and moving things, however, partnership with the responsible worker is only the *best* way to increase productivity. After all, Taylor's telling worked too, and quite well. In knowledge and service work, partnership with the responsible worker is the *only* way.

The last component of working smarter is a two-part lesson that neither Taylor nor Mayo knew. First, continuous learning must accompany productivity gains. Redesigning a job and then teaching the worker the new way to do it, which is what Taylor did and taught, cannot by itself sustain ongoing learning. Training is only the beginning of learning. Indeed, as the Japanese can teach us (thanks to their ancient tradition of Zen), the greatest benefit of training comes not from learning something new but from doing better what we already do well.

Equally important is a related insight of the last few years: knowledge workers and service workers learn most when they teach. The best way to improve a star salesperson's productivity is to ask her to present "the secret of my success" at the company sales convention. The best way for the surgeon to improve his performance is to give a talk about it at the county medical society. We often hear it said that in the information age, every enterprise has to become a learning institution. It must become a teaching institution as well.

O N E H U N D R E D years ago, the signs of class conflict were unmistakable. What defused that conflict—and averted class war—was growth in the productivity of the industrial work force, something so unprecedented that even its prime mover, Frederick Taylor, had no term to describe it.

Today we know that productivity is the true source of competitive advantage. But what we must also realize is that it is the key to social stability as well. For that reason, achieving gains in service productivity comparable with those we have already achieved in manufacturing productivity must be a priority for managers throughout the developed world.

It is an economic truth that real incomes cannot be higher than productivity for any extended length of time. Unless the productivity of service workers rapidly improves, both the social and the economic position of that large group of people—whose numbers rival those of manufacturing workers at their peak—must steadily go down. At a minimum, this raises the prospect of economic stagnation; more ominously, it raises the prospect of social tensions unmatched since the early decades of the Industrial Revolution.

Conceivably, service workers could use their numerical strength to get higher wages than their economic contribution justifies. But this would only impoverish all of society, dragging everyone's real income down and sending unemployment up. Alternatively, the income of unskilled and semiskilled service workers could continue to fall in relation to the steadily rising wages of affluent knowledge workers. But this would lead to an even wider gulf between the two groups as well as to increasing polarization. In either case, service workers can only become increasingly bitter, alienated, and ready to see themselves as a class apart.

Fortunately, we are in a much better position than our ancestors were a century ago. We know what Marx and his contemporaries did not know: productivity can be raised. We also know how to raise it. And we know this best for the work where the social need is most urgent: unskilled and semiskilled service work—maintenance jobs in factories, schools, hospitals, and offices; counter jobs in restaurants and supermarkets; clerical jobs in insurance companies, banks, and businesses of all kinds. In essence, this is production work. And what we have learned during the past 100 years about increasing productivity applies to such work with a minimum of adaptation.

Further, a model of sorts exists in the steps some multinational maintenance companies have already taken to improve their employees' productivity. These U.S. and European employers have systematically applied the approach this article discusses to low-skilled service jobs. They have defined the task, concentrated work on it, defined performance, made the employee a partner in productivity improvement and the first source of ideas for it, and built continuous learning and continuing teaching into the job of every employee and work team. As a result, they have raised productivity substantially—in some cases even doubled it—which has allowed them to raise wages. As important, this process has also greatly raised the workers' self-respect and pride.

It is no coincidence that outside contractors achieved these improvements. Obtaining major productivity gains in production-type service work usually requires contracting it out to a company that has no other business, understands this work, respects it, and offers opportunities for low-skilled workers to advance (for example, to become local or regional managers). The organizations in which this work is being done, the hospitals that own the beds, for instance, or the colleges whose students need to be fed, neither understand it nor respect it enough to devote the time and hard work that are required to make it more productive.

The task is known and doable. But the urgency is great. To raise the productivity of service work, we cannot rely on government or on politics altogether. It is the task of managers and executives in businesses and nonprofit organizations. It is, in fact, the first social responsibility of management in the knowledge society.

12   Management and
the World's Work

WHEN MARX was beginning work on *Das Kapital* in the early 1850s, the phenomenon of management was unknown. So were the enterprises that managers run. The largest manufacturing company around was a Manchester, England cotton mill employing fewer than 300 people, owned by Marx's friend and collaborator Friedrich Engels. And in Engels's mill—one of the most profitable businesses of its day—there were no "managers," only first-line supervisors, or charge hands, who were workers themselves, each enforcing discipline over a handful of fellow "proletarians."

Rarely in human history has any institution emerged as fast as management or had as great an impact as quickly. In less than 150 years, management has transformed the social and economic fabric of the world's developed countries. It has created a global economy and set new rules for countries that would participate in that economy as equals. And it has itself been transformed.

To be sure, the fundamental task of management remains the same: to make people capable of joint performance by giving them common goals, common values, the right structure, and the ongoing training and development they need to perform and to respond to change. But the very meaning of this task has changed, if only because the performance of management has converted the work force from one composed largely of unskilled laborers to one of highly educated knowledge workers.

September–October 1988

Few executives are aware of the tremendous impact management has had. Indeed, a good many are like M. Jourdain, the character in Molière's *Le Bourgeois Gentilhomme,* who did not know that he spoke prose. They barely realize that they practice–or mispractice–management. As a result, they are ill-prepared for the tremendous challenges that come upon them. For the truly important problems managers face do not come from technology or politics. They do not originate outside of management and enterprise. They are problems caused by the very success of management itself.

Eighty years ago, on the threshold of World War I, when a few people were just becoming aware of management's existence, most people in developed countries (perhaps four out of every five) earned their living in three occupations. There were domestic servants–in Great Britain, the largest single occupation (a full third of all workers), but a very large group everywhere, even in the United States. There were farmers–usually family farmers, who accounted for more than half the working population in every country except England and Belgium. And finally, there were blue-collar workers in manufacturing industries–the fastest growing occupation and the one that by 1925 would embrace almost 40 percent of the U.S. labor force.

Today domestic servants have all but disappeared. Full-time farmers account for only 3 percent to 5 percent of the working population in the non-Communist, developed countries, even though farm production is four to five times what it was 80 years ago. Blue-collar manufacturing employment is rapidly moving down the same path as farming. Manual workers employed in manufacturing in the United States now make up only 18 percent of the total work force; by the end of the century, they are likely to account for 10 percent or so in the United States and elsewhere–with manufacturing production steadily rising and expected to be at least 50 percent higher. The largest single group, more than one-third of the total, consists of workers whom the U.S. Bureau of the Census calls "managerial and professional." And a larger proportion of the total adult population than ever before–almost two-thirds in the United States, for instance—is now gainfully employed in every developed, non-Communist country.

Management has been the main agent of this unprecedented transformation. For it is management that explains why, for the first time in human history, we can employ large numbers of knowledgeable, skilled people in productive work. No earlier society could do this. Indeed, no earlier society could support more than a handful of such people because, until quite recently, no one knew how to put people with different skills and knowledge together to achieve common goals. Eighteenth century China was the envy of contemporary Western intellectuals because it supplied more jobs for educated people than all of Europe did—some 20,000 per year. Yet today, the United States with a roughly comparable population produces nearly one million college graduates a year, most of whom have little difficulty finding well-paid employment. What enables us to employ them is management.

Knowledge, especially advanced knowledge, is always highly specialized. By itself it produces nothing. Yet a modern large business can usefully employ up to 10,000 highly knowledgeable people who possess up to 60 different fields of knowledge. Engineers of all sorts, designers, marketing experts, economists, statisticians, psychologists, planners, accountants, human resources people—all work together in a joint venture, and none would be effective without the managed enterprise that is business.

The question of which came first—the educational explosion of the last 100 years or the management that could put this knowledge to productive use—is moot. Modern management and modern enterprise clearly could not exist without the knowledge base that developed societies have built. But equally, it is management and management alone that makes all this knowledge and these knowledgeable people effective. The emergence of management has converted knowledge from a social ornament and luxury into what we now know to be the true capital of any economy.

And knowledge, in turn—instead of bricks and mortar—has become the center of capital investment. Japan invests a record 8 percent of its annual GNP in plant and equipment. But Japan invests at least twice as much in education, two-thirds in schools for the young, the rest in the training and teaching of adults (largely in the organizations that employ them). And the United States puts an even larger share—roughly 20 percent—of its much larger GNP into education and training. In the modern society of enterprise and management, knowledge is the primary resource and society's true wealth.

NOT MANY business leaders could have predicted this development back in 1870, when large enterprises like those we know today were beginning to take shape. The reason was not so much lack of foresight as lack of precedent. At that time, the only large permanent organization around was the army. Not surprisingly, therefore, its command-and-control structure became the model for the men who were putting together transcontinental railroads, steel mills, modern banks, and department stores.

The command model, with a very few at the top giving orders and a great many at the bottom obeying them, remained the norm for nearly 100 years. But it was never as static as its longevity might suggest. On the contrary, it began to change almost at once, as specialized knowledge of all sorts poured into enterprise. The first university-trained engineer in manufacturing industry was hired in Germany in 1867, and within five years he had built a research department. Other specialties followed suit, and by World War I the familiar typical functions of a manufacturer had been developed: research and engineering, manufacturing, sales, finance and accounting, and a little later, human resources.

Even more important for its impact on enterprise—and on the world economy in general—was another management-directed development that took place at this time. That was the application of management to manual work in the form of training. The child of wartime necessity, training has propelled the transformation of the world economy in the last 30 years because it allows low-wage countries to do something that traditional economic theory had said could never be done: to become efficient—and yet still low-wage—competitors almost overnight.

Until World War I, it was axiomatic that it took a long time (Adam Smith said several hundred years) for a country or region to develop a tradition of labor and the expertise in manual and organizational skills needed to produce and market a given product, whether cotton textiles or violins. But during World War I, large numbers of totally unskilled, preindustrial people had to be made productive workers in practically no time. To meet this need, businesses in the United States and the United Kingdom began to apply Frederick Taylor's principles of "scientific management," developed between 1885 and 1910, to the systematic training of blue-collar workers on a large scale. They analyzed tasks and broke them down into individual, unskilled operations that could then be learned quite quickly. Further developed in World War II, training was then picked up by the Japanese and, 20 years later, by the South Koreans, who made it the basis for their countries' phenomenal development.

During the 1920s and 1930s, management was applied to many more areas and aspects of manufacturing business. Decentralization, for instance, arose to combine the advantages of bigness and the advantages of smallness within one enterprise. Accounting went from "bookkeeping" to analysis and control. Planning grew out of the "Gantt charts" designed in 1917 and 1918 to plan war production, and so did the use of analytical logic and statistics, which used quantification to convert experience and intuition into definitions, information, and diagnosis. Marketing similarly evolved as a result of applying management concepts to distribution and selling.

Moreover, as early as the mid-1920s and early 1930s, some management pioneers (Thomas Watson, Sr. at the fledgling IBM, General Robert E. Wood at Sears, Roebuck, and Elton Mayo at the Harvard Business School among them) began to question the way that manufacturing was organized. Eventually, they concluded that the assembly line was a short-term compromise despite its tremendous productivity: poor economics because of its inflexibility, poor use of human resources, even poor engineering. And so they began the thinking that eventually led to "automation" as the way to organize the manufacturing process, and to "Theory Y," teamwork, quality circles, and the information-based organization as the way to manage human resources.

Every one of these managerial innovations represented the application of knowledge to work, the substitution of system and information for guesswork, brawn, and toil. Every one, to use Frederick Taylor's terms, replaced "working harder" with "working smarter."

THE POWERFUL effect of these changes became apparent during World War II. To the very end, the Germans were by far the better strategists. And because they had the benefit of much shorter interior lines, they needed far fewer support troops and could match their opponents in combat strength. Yet the Allies won–their victory achieved by management.

The United States, with one-fifth the population, had almost as many men in uniform as all the other belligerents together. Yet it still produced more war material than all the others taken together. And it managed to get that material to fighting fronts as far apart as China, Russia, India, Africa, and Western Europe. No wonder, then, that by the war's end almost all the world had become management conscious. Or that management emerged as a recognizably distinct kind of work, one that could be studied and developed into a discipline–as happened in each of the countries that has exercised economic leadership during the postwar period.

But also, after World War II we began slowly to see that management is not *business* management. It pertains to every human effort that brings together in one organization people of diverse knowledge and skills. And it can be powerfully applied in hospitals, universities, churches, arts organizations, and social service agencies of all kinds. These "third sector" institutions have grown faster than either business or government in the developed countries since World War II. And their leaders are becoming more and more management conscious. For even though the need to manage volunteers or raise funds may differentiate nonprofit managers from their for-profit peers, many more of their responsibilities are the same–among them, defining the right strategy and goals, developing people, measuring performance, and marketing the organization's services.

This is not to say that our knowledge of management is complete. Management education today is on the receiving end of a great deal of criticism, much of it justified. What we knew about management 40 years ago–and have codified in our systems of organized management education–does not necessarily help managers meet the challenges they face today. Nevertheless, that knowledge was the foundation for the spectacular expansion the world economy has undergone since 1950, in developed and developing countries alike. And what has made that knowledge obsolete is, in large measure,

its own success in hastening the shift from manual work to knowledge work in business organizations.

To take just one example, we now have a great need for new
accounting concepts and methods. Experts like Robert Kaplan have
pointed out that many of the assumptions on which our system is
based are no longer valid.[1] For example, accounting conventions
assume that manufacturing industry is central; in fact, service and
information industries are now more important in all developed
countries. They also assume that a business produces just one product, whereas practically all modern businesses produce a great
many different products. But above all, cost accounting, that proud
invention of the mid-1920s, assumes that 80 percent of all costs
are attributable to direct manual labor. In reality, manual labor in
advanced manufacturing industries today accounts for no more than
8 percent to 12 percent of all costs. And the processes used in industries like automobiles and steel, in which labor costs are higher,
are distinctly antiquated.

Efforts to devise accounting systems that will reflect changes like
these—and provide accurate managerial information—are under way.
But they are still in the early stages. So are our efforts to find solutions
to other important management challenges: structures that work
for information-based organizations; ways to raise the productivity
of knowledge workers; techniques for managing existing businesses
and developing new and very different ones at the same time; ways
to build and manage truly global businesses; and many more.

M ANAGEMENT arose in developed countries. How does its rise
affect the developing world? Perhaps the best way to answer this
question is to start with the obvious: management and large enterprise, together with our new communications capacity, have created
a truly global economy. In the process, they have changed what
countries must do to participate effectively in that economy and to
achieve economic success.

In the past, starring roles in the world's economy were always
based on leadership in technological innovation. Great Britain became an economic power in the late eighteenth and early nineteenth
centuries through innovation in the steam engine, machine tools,

textiles, railroads, iron making, insurance, and international banking. Germany's economic star rose in the second half of the nineteenth century on innovation in chemistry, electricity, electronics, optics, steel, and the invention of the modern bank. The United States emerged as an economic power at the same time through innovative leadership in steel, electricity, telecommunications, electronics, automobiles, agronomy, office equipment, agricultural implements, and aviation.

But the one great economic power to emerge in this century—Japan—has not been a technological pioneer in any area. Its ascendancy rests squarely on leadership in management. The Japanese understood the lessons of America's managerial achievement during World War II more clearly than we did ourselves—especially with respect to managing people as a resource rather than as a cost. As a result, they adapted the West's new "social technology"—management—to make it fit their own values and traditions. They adopted (and adapted) organization theory to become the most thorough practitioners of decentralization in the world. (Pre-World War II Japan had been completely centralized.) And they began to practice marketing when most American companies were still only preaching it.

Japan also understood sooner than other countries that management and technology together had changed the economic landscape. The mechanical model of organization and technology, which came into being at the end of the seventeenth century when an obscure French physicist, Denis Papin, designed a prototypical steam engine, came to an end in 1945, when the first atomic bomb exploded and the first computer went on line. Since then, the model for both technology and organizations has been a biological one—interdependent, knowledge intensive, and organized by the flow of information.

One consequence of this change is that the industries that have been the carriers of enterprise for the last 100 years—industries like automobiles, steel, consumer electronics, and appliances—are in crisis. And this is true even where demographics seem to be in their favor. For example, countries like Mexico and Brazil have an abundant supply of young people who can be trained easily for semiskilled manual work. The mechanical industries would seem to be a perfect match. But as competitors in every industrial nation have found, mechanical production is antiquated unless it becomes automated—that is, unless it is restructured around information. For that reason alone, education is perhaps the greatest "management" challenge developing countries face.

Another way to arrive at the same conclusion is to look at a second fact with which developing countries must reckon: the developed countries no longer need them as they did during the nineteenth century. It may be hyperbole to say, as Japan's leading management consultant, Kenichi Ohmae, has said, that Japan, North America, and Western Europe can exist by themselves without the two-thirds of humanity who live in developing countries. But it is a fact that during the last 40 years the countries of this so called triad have become essentially self-sufficient except for petroleum. They produce more food than they can consume—in glaring contrast to the nineteenth century. They produce something like three-fourths of all the world's manufactured goods and services. And they provide the market for an equal proportion.

This poses an acute problem for developing countries, even very big ones like China and India. They cannot hope to become important economic powers by tracking the evolution of enterprise and management—that is, by starting with nineteenth and early twentieth century industries and productive processes based mainly on a manual work force. Demographically they may have no choice, of course. And maybe they can even begin to catch up. But can they ever get ahead? I doubt it.

During the last 200 years, no country has become a major economic power by following in the footsteps of earlier leaders. Each started out with what were, at the time, advanced industries and advanced production and distribution processes. And each, very fast, became a leader in management. Today, however, in part because of automation information and advanced technology, but in much larger part because of the demand for trained people in all areas of management, development requires a knowledge base that few developing countries possess or can afford. How to create an adequate managerial knowledge base fast is the critical question in economic development today. It is also one for which we have no answer so far.

Th e p r o b l e m s and challenges discussed so far are largely internal to management and enterprise. But the most important challenge ahead for management in developed countries is the result of an external change that I first called "pension fund socialism" in my 1976 book, *The Unseen Revolution: How Pension Fund Socialism Came to America*. I am referring, of course, to the shift of the titles of ownership of public companies to the institutional trustees of the country's employees, chiefly through their pension funds.

Socially this is the most positive development of the twentieth century because it resolves the "Social Question" that vexed the nineteenth century–the conflict between "capital" and "labor"–by merging the two. But it has also created the most violent turbulence for management and managers since they arose a century ago. For pension funds are the ultimate cause of the explosion of hostile takeovers in the last few years; and nothing has so disturbed and demoralized managers as the hostile takeover. In this sense, takeovers are only a symptom of the fundamental questions pension fund socialism raises about the legitimacy of management: To whom are managers accountable? For what? What is the purpose and rationale of large, publicly owned enterprises?

In 1986, the last year for which we have figures, the pension funds of America's employees owned more than 40 percent of U.S. companies' equity capital and more than two-thirds of the equity capital of the 1,000 largest companies. The funds of large institutions (businesses, states, cities, public service and nonprofit institutions like universities, school districts, and hospitals) accounted for three-quarters of these holdings. The funds of individuals (employees of small businesses and the self-employed) accounted for the other fourth. (Mutual funds, which also represent the savings of wage earners rather than of "capitalists," hold another 5 percent to 10 percent of the country's equity capital.)

These figures mean that pension funds are already the primary suppliers of capital in the United States. Indeed, it is almost impossible to build a new business or expand an existing one unless pension-fund money is available. In the next few years, the funds' holdings will become even larger, if only because federal government employees now have a pension fund that invests in equity shares. Thus, by the year 2000, pension funds will hold at least two-thirds of the share capital of all U.S. businesses except the smallest. Through their pension funds, U.S. employees will be the true owners of the country's means of production.

The same development, with a lag of about ten years, is taking place in Great Britain, Japan, West Germany, and Sweden. It is also starting to appear in France, Italy, and the Netherlands.

This startling development was not foreseen, but it was inevitable—the result of several interdependent factors. First is the shift in income distribution that directs 90 percent or so of the GNP in non-Communist, developed countries into the wage fund. (The figure varies from 85 percent in the United States to 95 percent or more in the Netherlands and Denmark.) Indeed, economically the "rich" have become irrelevant in developed countries, however much they dominate the society pages and titillate TV viewers. Even the very rich have actually become much poorer in this century if their incomes are adjusted for inflation and taxation. To be in the same league as the "tycoon" of 1900, today's "super-rich" person would need a net worth of at least $50 billion—perhaps even $100 billion—and income to match. A few Arab sheiks may qualify, but surely no one in a developed country.

At the same time, wage earners' real incomes have risen dramatically. Few employees in turn-of-the-century America could lay aside anything beyond their mortgage payments or the premiums on funeral insurance. But since then, the American industrial worker's real income and purchasing power have grown more than 20 times larger, even though the number of hours worked has dropped by 50 percent. The same has occurred in all the other industrially developed countries. And it has happened fastest in Japan, where the real income of industrial workers may now be as much as 30 times what it was 80 years ago.

Demand for this income is essentially limitless because we are again in the midst of an intensively creative period. In the 60 years between 1856 and World War I, a technical or social innovation that led almost immediately to a new industry appeared, on average, once every 14 months. And this entrepreneurial explosion underlay the rise of the tycoons. We needed people like J. P. Morgan, John D. Rockefeller, Sr., Andrew Carnegie, Friedrich Krupp, and the Mitsui family who could finance whole industries out of their private pockets. Technical and social innovations are coming just as fast today. And the effect of all this energy is that companies and countries require enormous amounts of capital just to keep up, let alone move ahead–amounts that are several orders of magnitude larger than those the tycoons had to supply 80 years ago.

Indeed, the total pretax incomes of America's 1,000 highest income earners would be barely adequate to cover the capital needs of the country's private industry for more than three or four days. This holds true for all developed countries. In Japan, for instance, the pretax incomes of the country's 2,000 highest income earners just about equals what the country's private industry invests every two or three days.

These economic developments would have forced us in any event to make workers into "capitalists" and owners of productive resources. That pension funds became the vehicle–rather than mutual funds or direct individual investments in equity as everyone expected 30 years ago–is the result of the demographic shift that has raised life expectancies in developed countries from age 40 to the mid- and late-70s. The number of older people is much too large, and the years during which they need an income too many, for them to depend on support from their children. They must rely on monies they themselves have put aside during their earning years–and these funds have to be invested for long stretches of time.

THAT MODERN society requires an identity of interest between enterprise and employee was seen very early, not only by pre-Marxist socialists like Saint-Simon and Fourier in France and Robert Owen in Scotland but also by classical economists like Adam Smith and David Ricardo. Attempts to satisfy this need through worker ownership of business thus go back more than 150 years. Without exception, they have failed.

In the first place, worker ownership does not satisfy the workers' basic financial and economic needs. It puts all the workers' financial resources into the business that employs them. But the workers' needs are primarily long-term, particularly the need for retirement income many years hence. So to be a sound investment for its worker-owners, a business has to prosper for a very long time–and only one business out of every 40 or 50 ever does. Indeed, few even survive long enough. But worker ownership also *destroys* companies in the end because it always leads to inadequate capital formation, inadequate investment in research and development, and stubborn resistance to abandonment of outmoded, unproductive, and obsolete products, processes, plants, jobs, and work rules.

Zeiss Optical Works, the oldest worker-owned business around, lost its leadership position in consumer optics to the Americans and the Japanese for just this reason. Time and again, Zeiss's worker-owners preferred immediate satisfaction–higher wages, bonuses, benefits–to investing in research, new products, and new markets. Worker ownership underlies the near collapse of industry in contemporary Yugoslavia. And its shortcomings are so greatly hampering industry in China that the country's leaders are trying to shift to "contract management," which will expand managerial autonomy and check the power of "work councils" and worker-owners.

And yet, worker ownership of the means of production is not only a sound concept, it is also inevitable. Power follows property, says the old axiom. Both James Madison, in the *Federalist Papers*, and Karl Marx took it from the seventeenth century English philosopher, James Harrington, who in turn took it from Aristotle. It can be found in early Confucian writings as well. And since property has shifted to the wage earners in all developed countries, power has to follow. Yet unlike any other worker ownership of the means of production, pension fund socialism maintains the autonomy and accountability of enterprise and management, market freedom, competition, and the ability to change and to innovate.

But pension fund socialism does not function fully as yet. We can solve the financial and economic problems it presents. We know, for instance, that a pension fund must invest no more than a small fraction of its assets, 5 percent perhaps, in the shares of its own company or of any one company altogether. We know quite a bit, though not nearly enough, about how to invest pension fund money. But we still have to solve the basic sociopolitical problem: how to build the accomplished fact of employee ownership into the governance of both pension funds and businesses.

Pᴇɴsɪᴏɴ ғᴜɴᴅs are the legal owners of the companies in which they invest. But they not only have no "ownership interest"; as trustees for the ultimate beneficiaries, the employees, they also are legally obligated to be nothing but "investors," and short-term investors at that. That is why it is worker ownership that has made the hostile takeover possible. For as trustees, the pension funds must sell if someone bids more than the market price.

Whether hostile takeovers benefit shareholders is a hotly debated issue. That they have serious economic side effects is beyond question. The fear of a hostile takeover may not be the only reason American managements tend to subordinate everything–market standing, research, product development, service, quality, innovation–to the short term. But it is surely a major reason. Moreover, the hostile takeover is a frontal attack on management and managers. Indeed, what makes the mere threat of a takeover so demoralizing to managers (especially the middle managers and professionals on whom a business depends for its performance) is the raiders' barely concealed contempt, which management sees as contempt for wealth-producing work, and their work's subordination to financial manipulation.

For their part, the raiders and their financial backers maintain that management is solely accountable to the shareholders *whatever* their wishes, even if those represent nothing more than short-term speculative gains and asset stripping. This is indeed what the law says. But the law was written for early nineteenth century business conditions, well before large enterprise and management came into being. And while every free-market country has similar laws, not all countries hold to them. In Japan, for instance, custom dictates that larger companies exist mainly for the sake of their employees except in the event of bankruptcy; and Japanese economic performance and even Japanese shareholders have surely not suffered as a result. In West Germany too, large enterprises are seen as "going concerns," whose preservation is in the national interest and comes before shareholders' gains.

Both Japan and Germany have organized an extra-legal but highly effective way to hold business managements accountable, however, in the form of the voting control exercised by the big commercial banks of both countries. No such system exists in the United States (or the United Kingdom), nor could it possibly be constructed. And even in Japan and Germany, the hold of the banks is weakening fast.

So we must think through what management should be accountable for; and how and through whom its accountability can be discharged. The stockholders' interest, both short- and long-term, is one of the areas, to be sure. But it is only one.

One thing is clear to anyone with the slightest knowledge of political or economic history: the present-day assertion of "absolute shareholder sovereignty" (of which the boom in takeovers is the most spectacular manifestation) is the last hurrah of nineteenth century, basically preindustrial capitalism. It violates many people's sense of justice–as the upsurge of "populism" and anti-Wall Street rhetoric in the 1988 presidential campaign attest.

But even more important, no economy can perform if it puts what Thorstein Veblen, some 70 years ago, called "the acquisitive instinct" ahead of the "instinct of workmanship." Modern enterprise, especially large enterprise, can do its economic job–including making profits for the shareholders–only if it is being managed for the long run. Investments, whether in people, in products, in plants, in processing, in technology, or in markets, require several years of gestation before there is even a "baby," let alone full-grown results. Altogether far too much in society–jobs, careers, communities–depends on the economic fortunes of large enterprises to subordinate them completely to the interests of any one group, including shareholders.

How to make the interests of shareholders–and this means pension funds–compatible with the needs of the economy and society is thus the big issue pension fund socialism has to resolve. And it has to be done in a way that makes managements accountable, especially for economic and financial performance, and yet allows them to manage for the long term. How we answer this challenge will decide both the shape and place of management and the structure, if not the survival, of the free-market economy. It will also detemine America's ability to compete in a world economy in which competitive long-range strategies are more and more the norm.

Finally, what is management? Is it a bag of techniques and tricks? A bundle of analytical tools like those taught in business schools? These are important, to be sure, just as the thermometer and a knowledge of anatomy are important to the physician. But what the evolution and history of management—its successes as well as its problems—teach is that management is, above all else, a very few, essential principles. To be specific:

1. Management is about human beings. Its task is to make people capable of joint performance, to make their strengths effective and their weaknesses irrelevant. This is what organization is all about, and it is the reason that management is the critical, determining factor. These days, practically all of us are employed by managed institutions, large and small, business and nonbusiness—and that is especially true for educated people. We depend on management for our livelihoods and our ability to contribute and achieve. Indeed, our ability to contribute to society at all usually depends as much on the management of the enterprises in which we work as it does on our own skills, dedication, and effort.

2. Because management deals with the integration of people in a common venture, it is deeply embedded in culture. What managers do in West Germany, in Britain, in the United States, in Japan, or in Brazil is exactly the same. How they do it may be quite different. Thus one of the basic challenges managers in a developing country face is to find and identify those parts of their own tradition, history, and culture that can be used as building blocks. The difference between Japan's economic success and India's relative backwardness, for instance, is largely explained by the fact that Japanese managers were able to plant imported management concepts in their own cultural soil and make them grow. Whether China's leaders can do the same—or whether their great tradition will become an impediment to the country's development—remains to be seen.

3. Every enterprise requires simple, clear, and unifying objectives. Its mission has to be clear enough and big enough to provide a common vision. The goals that embody it have to be clear, public, and often reaffirmed. We hear a great deal of talk these days about the "culture" of an organization. But what we really mean by this is the commitment throughout an enterprise to some common objectives and common values. Without such

commitment there is no enterprise; there is only a mob. Management's job is to think through, set, and exemplify those objectives, values, and goals.

4. It is also management's job to enable the enterprise and each of its members to grow and develop as needs and opportunities change. This means that every enterprise is a learning and teaching institution. Training and development must be built into it on all levels—training and development that never stop.

5. Every enterprise is composed of people with different skills and knowledge doing many different kinds of work. For that reason, it must be built on communication and on individual responsibility. Each member has to think through what he or she aims to accomplish—and make sure that associates know and understand that aim. Each has to think through what he or she owes to others—and make sure that others understand and approve. Each has to think through what is needed from others—and make sure that others know what is expected of them.

6. Neither the quantity of output nor the bottom line is by itself an adequate measure of the performance of management and enterprise. Market standing, innovation, productivity, development of people, quality, financial results—all are crucial to a company's performance and indeed to its survival. In this respect, an enterprise is like a human being. Just as we need a diversity of measures to assess the health and performance of a person, we need a diversity of measures for an enterprise. Performance has to be built into the enterprise and its management; it has to be measured—or at least judged—and it has to be continuously improved.

7. Finally, the single most important thing to remember about any enterprise is that there are no results inside its walls. The result of a business is a satisfied customer. The result of a hospital is a healed patient. The result of a school is a student who has learned something and puts it to work ten years later. Inside an enterprise, there are only cost centers. Results exist only on the outside.

About management, as about any other area of human work, much more could be said. Tools must be acquired and used. Techniques and any number of processes and procedures must be learned. But managers who truly understand the principles outlined above and truly manage themselves in their light will be achieving, accomplished managers–the kind of managers who build successful, productive, and achieving enterprises all over the world and who establish standards, set examples, and leave as a legacy both greater capacity to produce wealth and greater human vision.

13 The Post-Capitalist Executive

An Interview with Peter F. Drucker
by T. George Harris

T. GEORGE HARRIS, a Drucker collaborator for 24 years, went to the Drucker Management Center at the Claremont Graduate School in California for two days of intensive conversation about the practical implications of Peter Drucker's book *Post-Capitalist Society* (Harper Collins, 1993) for today's executives.

Harris: *Peter, you always bring ideas down to the gut level where people work and live. Now we need to know how managers can operate in the post-capitalist society.*

Peter F. Drucker: You have to learn to manage in situations where you don't have command authority, where you are neither controlled nor controlling. That is the fundamental change. Management textbooks still talk mainly about managing subordinates. But you no longer evaluate an executive in terms of how many people report to him or her. That standard doesn't mean as much as the complexity of the job, the information it uses and generates, and the different kinds of relationships needed to do the work.

May–June 1993

Similarly, business news still refers to managing subsidiaries. But this is the control approach of the 1950s or 1960s. The reality is that the multinational corporation is rapidly becoming an endangered species. Businesses used to grow in one of two ways: from grassroots up or by acquisition. In both cases, the manager had control. Today businesses grow through alliances, all kinds of dangerous liaisons and joint ventures, which, by the way, very few people understand. This new type of growth upsets the traditional manager who believes he or she must own or control sources and markets.

How will the manager operate in a work environment free of the old hierarchies?

Would you believe that you're going to work permanently with people who work for you but are not your employees? Increasingly, for instance, you outsource when possible. It is predictable, then, that ten years from now a company will outsource all work that does not have a career ladder up to senior management. To get productivity, you have to outsource activities that have their own senior management. Believe me, the trend toward outsourcing has very little to do with economizing and a great deal to do with quality.

Can you give an example?

Take a hospital. Everybody there knows how important cleanliness is, but doctors and nurses are never going to be very concerned with how you sweep in corners. That's not part of their value system. They need a hospital maintenance company. One company I got to know in Southern California had a cleaning woman who came in as an illiterate Latino immigrant. She is brilliant. She figured out how to split a bed sheet so that the bed of a very sick patient, no matter how heavy, could be changed. Using her method, you have to move the patient about only six inches, and she cut the bed-making time from twelve minutes to two. Now she's in charge of the cleaning operations, but she is not an employee of the hospital. The hospital can't give her one single order. It can only say, "We don't like this; we'll work it out."

The point is, managers still talk about the people who "report" to them, but that word should be stricken from management vocabulary. Information is replacing authority. A company treasurer with outsourced information technology (IT) may have only two assistants and a receptionist, but his decisions in foreign exchange can lose—or make—more money in a day than the rest of the company makes all year. A scientist decides which research *not* to do in a big company lab. He doesn't even have a secretary or a title, but his track record means that he is not apt to be overruled. He may have more effect than the CEO. In the military, a lieutenant colonel used to command a battalion, but today he may have only a receptionist and be in charge of liaisons with a major foreign country.

Amidst these new circumstances, everybody is trying to build the ideal organization, generally flat with few layers of bosses and driven directly by consumer satisfaction. But how do managers gear up their lives for this new world?

More than anything else, the individual has to take more responsibility for himself or herself, rather than depend on the company. In this country, and beginning in Europe and even Japan, you can't expect that if you've worked for a company for five years you'll be there when you retire 40 years from now. Nor can you expect that you will be able to do what you want to do at the company in 40 years time. In fact, if you make a wager on any big company, the chances of it being split within the next 10 years are better than the chances of it remaining the way it is.

This is a new trend. Big corporations became stable factors before World War I and in the 1920s were almost frozen. Many survived the Depression without change. Then there were 30 or 40 years when additional stories were built onto skyscrapers or more wings added onto corporate centers. But now they're not going to build corporate skyscrapers. In fact, within the past ten years, the proportion of the work force employed by *Fortune* "500" companies has fallen from 30 percent to 13 percent.

Corporations once built to last like pyramids are now more like tents. Tomorrow they're gone or in turmoil. And this is true not only of companies in the headlines like Sears or GM or IBM. Technology is changing very quickly, as are markets and structures. You can't design your life around a temporary organization.

Let me give you a simple example of the way assumptions are changing. Most men and women in the executive program I teach are about 45 years old and just below senior management in a big organization or running a midsize one. When we began 15 or 20 years ago, people at this stage were asking, "How can we prepare ourselves for the next promotion?" Now they say, "What do I need to learn so that I can decide where to go next?"

If a young man in a gray flannel suit represented the lifelong corporate type, what's today's image?

Taking individual responsibility and not depending on any particular company. Equally important is managing your own career. The stepladder is gone, and there's not even the implied structure of an industry's rope ladder. It's more like vines, and you bring your own machete. You don't know what you'll be doing next, or whether you'll work in a private office or one big amphitheater or even out of your home. You have to take responsibility for knowing yourself, so you can find the right jobs as you develop and as your family becomes a factor in your values and choices.

That's a significant departure from what managers could expect in the past.

Well, the changes in the manager's work are appearing everywhere, though on different timetables. For instance, I see more career confusion among the many Japanese students I've had over the years. They're totally bewildered. Though they are more structured than we ever were, suddenly the Japanese are halfway between being totally managed and having to take responsibility for themselves. What frightens them is that titles don't mean what they used to mean. Whether you were in India or France, if you were an assistant director of market research, everybody used to know what you were doing. That's not true any more, as we found in one multinational. A woman who had just completed a management course told me not long ago that in five years she would be an assistant vice president of her bank. I'm afraid I had to tell her that she might indeed get the title, but it would no longer have the meaning she thought it did.

Another rung in the ladder?

Yes. The big-company mentality. Most people expect the personnel department to be Papa or Ma Bell. When the AT&T personnel department was at its high point 30 years ago, it was the power behind the scenes. With all their testing and career planning, they'd know that a particular 27-year-old would be, by age 45, an assistant operating manager and no more. They didn't know whether he'd be in Nebraska or Florida. But unless he did something quite extraordinary, his career path until retirement was set.

Times have certainly changed. And, in fact, the Bell people have done better than most, because they could see that change coming in the antitrust decision. They couldn't ignore it. But most people still have a big-company mentality buried in their assumptions. If they lose a job with Sears, they hunt for one with Kmart, unaware that small companies create most of the new jobs and are about as secure as big companies.

Even today, remarkably few Americans are prepared to select jobs for themselves. When you ask, "Do you know what you are good at? Do you know your limitations?" they look at you with a blank stare. Or they often respond in terms of subject knowledge, which is the wrong answer. When they prepare their resumes, they still try to list positions like steps up a ladder. It is time to give up thinking of jobs or career paths as we once did and think in terms of taking on assignments one after the other.

How does one prepare for this new kind of managerial career?

Being an educated person is no longer adequate, not even educated in management. One hears that the government is doing research on new job descriptions based on subject knowledge. But I think that we probably have to leap right over the search for objective criteria and get into the subjective—what I call *competencies*. Do you really like pressure? Can you be steady when things are rough and confused? Do you absorb information better by reading, talking, or looking at graphs and numbers? I asked one executive the other day, "When you sit down with a person, a subordinate, do you know what to say?" Empathy is a practical competence. I have been urging this kind of self-knowledge for years, but now it is essential for survival.

People, especially the young, think that they want all the freedom they can get, but it is very demanding, very difficult to think through who you are and what you do best. In helping people learn how to be responsible, our educational system is more and more counter-productive. The longer you stay in school, the fewer decisions you have to make. For instance, the decision whether to take French II or art history is really based on whether one likes to get up early in the morning. And graduate school is much worse.

Do you know why most people start with big companies? Because most graduates have not figured out where to place themselves, and companies send in the recruiters. But as soon as the recruits get through training and into a job, they have to start making decisions about the future. Nobody's going to do it for them.

And once they start making decisions, many of the best move to midsize companies in three to five years, because there they can break through to top management. With less emphasis on seniority, a person can go upstairs and say, "I've been in accounting for three years, and I'm ready to go into marketing." Each year I phone a list of my old students to see what's happening with them. The second job used to be with another big company, often because people were beginning to have families and wanted security. But with two-career families, a different problem emerges. At a smaller organization, you can often work out arrangements for both the man and the woman to move to new jobs in the same city.

Some of the psychological tests being developed now are getting better at helping people figure out their competencies. But if the world economy is shifting from a command model to a knowledge model, why shouldn't education determine who gets each job?

Because of the enormous danger that we would not value the person in terms of performance, but in terms of credentials. Strange as it may seem, a knowledge economy's greatest pitfall is in becoming a Mandarin meritocracy. You see creeping credentialism all around. Why should people find it necessary to tell me so-and-so is really a good researcher even though he or she doesn't have a Ph.D.? It's easy to fall into the trap because degrees are black-and-white. But it takes judgment to weigh a person's contribution.

The problem is becoming more serious in information-based organizations. As Michael Hammer pointed out three years ago in *Harvard Business Review,* when an organization reengineers itself around information, the majority of management layers becomes redundant. Most turn out to have been just information relays. Now, each layer has much more information responsibility. Most large companies have cut the number of layers by 50 percent, even in Japan. Toyota came down from 20-odd to eleven. GM has streamlined from 28 to maybe 19, and even that number is decreasing rapidly. Organizations will become flatter and flatter.

As a result, there's real panic in Japan, because it's a vertical society based on subtle layers of status. Everybody wants to become a *kachō*, a supervisor or section manager. Still, the United States doesn't have the answer either. We don't know how to use rewards and recognition to move the competent people into the management positions that remain. I don't care for the popular theory that a generation of entrepreneurs can solve our problems. Entrepreneurs are monomaniacs. Managers are synthesizers who bring resources together and have that ability to "smell" opportunity and timing. Today perception is more important than analysis. In the new society of organizations, you need to be able to recognize patterns to see what is there rather than what you expect to see. You need the invaluable listener who says, "I hear us all trying to kill the new product to protect the old one."

How do you find these people?

One way is to use small companies as farm clubs, as in baseball. One of my ablest friends is buying minority stakes in small companies within his industry. When I said it didn't make sense, he said, "I'm buying farm teams. I'm putting my bright young people in these companies so they have their own commands. They have to do everything a CEO does in a big company."

And do you know the biggest thing these young executives have to learn in their new positions? My friend continued, "We have more Ph.D.'s in biology and chemistry than we have janitors, and they have to learn that their customers aren't Ph.D.'s, and the people who do the work aren't." In other words, they must learn to speak English instead of putting formulas on the blackboard. They must learn to listen to somebody who does not know what a regression analysis is. Basically, they have to learn the meaning and importance of respect.

A difficult thing to learn, let alone teach.

You have to focus on a person's performance. The individual must shoulder the burden of defining what his or her own contribution will be. We have to demand–and "demand" is the word, nothing permissive–that people think through what constitutes the greatest contribution that they can make to the company in the next eighteen months or two years. Then they have to make sure that contribution is accepted and understood by the people they work with and for.

Most people don't ask themselves this question, however obvious and essential it seems. When I ask people what they contribute to an organization, they blossom and love to answer. And when I follow with, "Have you told other people about it?" the answer often is "No, that would be silly because they know." But of course "they" don't. We are 100 years past the simple economy in which most people knew what others did at work. Farmers knew what most farmers did, and industrial workers knew what other factory workers did. Domestic servants understood each other's work, as did the fourth major group in that economy: small tradesmen. No one needed to explain. But now nobody knows what others do, even within the same organization. Everybody you work with needs to know your priorities. If you don't ask and don't tell, your peers and subordinates will guess incorrectly.

What's the result of this lack of communication?

When you don't communicate, you don't get to do the things you are good at. Let me give you an example. The engineers in my class, without exception, say they spend more than half their time editing and polishing reports–in other words, what they are least qualified to do. They don't even know that you have to write and rewrite and rewrite again. But there are any number of English majors around for that assignment. People seldom pay attention to their strengths. For example, after thinking for a long time, an engineer told me he's really good at the first design, at the basic idea, but not at filling in the details for the final product. Until then, he'd never told anybody, not even himself.

You're not advocating self-analysis alone, are you?

No. You not only have to understand your own competencies, but you also have to learn the strengths of the men and women to whom you assign duties, as well as those of your peers and boss. Too many managers still go by averages. They still talk about "our engineers." And I say, "Brother, you don't have engineers. You have Joe and Mary and Jim and Bob, and each is different." You can no longer manage a work force. You manage individuals. You have to know them so well you can go and say, "Mary, you think you ought to move up to this next job. Well, then you have to learn not to have that chip on your shoulder. Forget you are a woman; you are an engineer. And you have to be a little considerate. Do not come in at ten minutes to five on Friday afternoon to tell people they have to work overtime when you knew it at 9 A.M."

The key to the productivity of knowledge workers is to make them concentrate on the real assignment. Do you know why most promotions now fail? One-third are outright disasters, in my experience, while another third are a nagging backache. Not more than one in three works out. No fit. The standard case, of course, is the star salesman promoted to sales manager. That job can be any one of four things–a manager of salespeople, a market manager, a brand manager, or a super salesman who opens up an entire new area. But nobody figures out what it is, so the man or woman who got the promotion just tries to do more of whatever led to the promotion. That's the surest way to be wrong.

Expand on your idea of information responsibility and how it fits into post-capitalist society.

Far too many managers think computer specialists know what information they need to do their job and what information they owe to whom. Computer information tends to focus too much on inside information, not the outside sources and customers that count. In today's organization, you have to take responsibility for information because it is your main tool. But most don't know how to use it. Few are information literate. They can play "Mary Had a Little Lamb" but not Beethoven.

I heard today about a brand manager in a major over-the-counter drug company who tried to get the scientific papers on the product he markets. But the corporate librarian complained to his superior. Under her rules, she gives hard science only to the company's scientists and lawyers. He had to get a consultant to go outside and use a computer database to pull up about 20 journal articles on his product, so he'd know how to develop honest advertising copy. The point of the story is that this brand manager is way ahead of the parade: 99 out of 100 brand managers don't know they need that kind of information for today's consumers and haven't a clue how to get it. The first step is to say, "I need it."

And many people don't recognize the importance of this step. I work with an information manager at a large financial institution that has invested $1.5 billion in information. He and I talked all morning with his department's eight women and ten men. Very intelligent, but not one began to think seriously about what information they need to serve their customers. When I pointed this out, they said, "Isn't the boss going to tell us?" We finally had to agree to meet a month later so that they could go through the hard work of figuring out what information they need and—more important—what they do not need.

So a manager begins the road to information responsibility first by identifying gaps in knowledge.

Exactly. To be information literate, you begin with learning what it is you need to know. Too much talk focuses on the technology, even worse on the speed of the gadget, always faster, faster. This kind of "techie" fixation causes us to lose track of the fundamental nature of information in today's organization. To organize the way work is done, you have to begin with the specific job, then the information input, and finally the human relationships needed to get the job done.

The current emphasis on reengineering essentially means changing an organization from the flow of things to the flow of information. The computer is merely a tool in the process. If you go to the hardware store to buy a hammer, you do not ask if you should do upholstery or fix the door. To put it in editorial terms, knowing how a typewriter works does not make you a writer. Now that knowledge is taking the place of capital as the driving force in organizations worldwide, it is all too easy to confuse data with knowledge and information technology with information.

What's the worst problem in managing knowledge specialists?

One of the most degenerative tendencies of the last 40 years is the belief that if you are understandable, you are vulgar. When I was growing up, it was taken for granted that economists, physicists, psychologists–leaders in any discipline–would make themselves understood. Einstein spent years with three different collaborators to make his theory of relativity accessible to the layman. Even John Maynard Keynes tried hard to make his economics accessible. But just the other day, I heard a senior scholar seriously reject a younger colleague's work because more than five people could understand what he's doing. Literally.

We cannot afford such arrogance. Knowledge is power, which is why people who had it in the past often tried to make a secret of it. In post-capitalism, power comes from transmitting information to make it productive, not from hiding it.

That means you have to be intolerant of intellectual arrogance. And I mean intolerant. At whatever level, knowledge people must make themselves understood, and whatever field the manager comes from, he or she must be eager to understand others. This may be the main job of the manager of technical people. He or she must not only be an interpreter but also work out a balance between specialization and exposure.

Exposure is an important technique. For an exotic example, look at weather forecasting, where meteorologists and mathematicians and other specialists now work with teams of experts on satellite data. Europeans, on the one hand, have tried to connect these different disciplines entirely through information managers. On the other hand, Americans rotate people at an early stage. Suppose you put a Ph.D. in meteorology on a team that is to work on the new mathematical model of hurricanes for three years. He isn't a mathematician, but he gets exposed to what mathematicians assume, what they eliminate, what their limitations are. With the combination of exposure and translation, the American approach yields forecasts that are about three times more accurate than the European, I'm told. And the exposure concept is useful in managing any group of specialists.

Is the fact that some teams provide exposure as well as interpreters a reason why the team has become such a hot topic?

There's a lot of nonsense in team talk, as if teams were something new. We have always worked in teams, and while sports give us hundreds of team styles there are only a few basic models to choose from. The critical decision is to select the right kind for the job. You can't mix soccer and doubles tennis. It's predictable that in a few years, the most traditional team will come back in fashion, the one that does research first, then passes the idea to engineering to develop, and then on to manufacturing to make. It's like a baseball team, and you may know I have done a little work with baseball-team management.

The great strength of baseball teams is that you can concentrate. You take Joe, who is a batter, and you work on batting. There is almost no interaction, nothing at all like the soccer team or the jazz combo, the implicit model of many teams today. The soccer team moves in unison but everyone holds the same relative position. The jazz combo has incredible flexibility because everyone knows each other so well that they all sense when the trumpet is about to solo. The combo model takes great discipline and may eventually fall out of favor, especially in Japanese car manufacturing, because we do not need to create new models as fast as we have been.

I know several German companies that follow the baseball-team model, whether they know it or not. Their strength is clear: they are fantastic at exploiting and developing old knowledge, and Germany's midsize companies may be better than their big ones simply because they concentrate better. On the other hand, when it comes to the new, from electronics to biotech, German scientists may do fine work, but their famous apprenticeship system discourages innovation.

So, beyond all the hype, teams can help the executive navigate a post-capitalist society?

Thinking about teams helps us highlight the more general problem of how to manage knowledge. In the production of fundamental new knowledge, the British groups I run into are way ahead of anybody. But they have never done much with their expertise, in part because many British companies don't value the technically oriented person enough. I don't know of a single engineer in top management there. My Japanese friends are just the opposite. While they still do not specialize in scientific advances, they take knowledge and make it productive very fast. In this country, on the other hand, we have not improved that much in existing industries. The automobile business, until recently, was perfectly satisfied doing what it did in 1939. But, as we are discovering in computers and in biotech, we may be at our very best when it comes to groundbreaking technology.

Where is the lesson in all this for the manager?

The lesson is that the productivity of knowledge has both a qualitative and a quantitative dimension. Though we know very little about it, we do realize executives must be both managers of specialists and synthesizers of different fields of knowledge—really of knowledges, plural. This situation is as threatening to the traditional manager, who worries about high-falutin' highbrows, as it is to the intellectual, who worries about being too commercial to earn respect in his or her discipline. But in the post-capitalist world, the highbrow and the lowbrow have to play on the same team.

That sounds pretty democratic. Does a post-capitalist society based more on knowledge than capital become egalitarian?

No. Both of these words miss the point. *Democratic* bespeaks a narrow political and legal organization. Nor do I use the buzzword *participative.* Worse yet is the *empowerment* concept. It is not a great step forward to take power out at the top and put it in at the bottom. It's still power. To build achieving organizations, you must replace power with responsibility.

And, while we're on the subject of words, I'm not comfortable with the word *manager* any more, because it implies subordinates. I find myself using *executive* more, because it implies responsibility for an area, not necessarily dominion over people. The word *boss,* which emerged in World War II, is helpful in that it can be used to suggest a mentor's role, someone who can back you up on a decision. The new organizations need to go beyond senior and junior polarities to a blend with sponsor and mentor relations. In the traditional organization–the organization of the last 100 years–the skeleton, or internal structure, was a combination of rank and power. In the emerging organization, it has to be mutual understanding and responsibility.

Notes

Introduction

1. There is no better–or more enjoyable–way to learn how Drucker came to be a student of management at GM than to read *Adventures of a Bystander* (New York: Harper & Row, 1979), his memoir of the people and events that helped to shape his vision of the world (and the book from which the quotations in the introduction come). The topics of his essays have ranged from his fourth-grade teachers in pre-World War I Vienna, to the merchant bankers of Freedberg & Co. in London, to encounters with personages like Sigmund Freud and Time-Life's Henry Luce. Drucker's enormous curiosity and intellectual energy, his powers of analysis and eye for telling details, his mistrust of received wisdom and penchant for unconventional choices are uniformly reflected in his works: in sum, these are the very qualities that distinguish his writing on management and that make so many of his books and articles worth not just reading–but re-reading as well.
2. Every year since 1959, an independent panel of CEOs and management thinkers has selected the most influential articles published in *Harvard Business Review* to receive awards from the McKinsey Foundation.
3. Interested readers will find a complete list of the articles Peter has published in *HBR* following this introduction.

Chapter 4

1. See Theodore Levitt, "Creativity Is Not Enough," *Harvard Business Review* 41, no. 3 (1963): 72.

Chapter 6

1. This was brought out clearly by J. Roger Morrison and Richard F. Neuschel, "The Second Squeeze on Profits," *Harvard Business Review* 40, no. 4 (1962): 49; see also Louis E. Newman and Sidney Brunell, "Different Dollars," *Harvard Business Review* 40, no. 4 (1962): 74.

2. Morrison and Neuschel, "Second Squeeze on Profits"; and John Dearden, "Profit-Planning Accounting for Small Firms," *Harvard Business Review* 41, no. 2 (1963): 66.

Chapter 7

1. James P. Womack and Daniel T. Jones, "From Lean Production to the Lean Enterprise," *Harvard Business Review* 72, no. 2 (1994): 93–103.
2. I discussed EVA at considerable length in my 1964 book, *Managing for Results,* but the last generation of classical economists, Alfred Marshall in England and Eugen Böhm-Bawerk in Austria, were already discussing it in the late 1890s.
3. C. K. Prahalad and Gary Hamel, "The Core Competence of the Corporation," *Harvard Business Review* 68, no. 3 (1990): 79–91.

Chapter 8

1. The standard account is Philip Woodruff, *The Men Who Ruled India,* especially the first volume, *The Founders of Modern India* (New York: St. Martin's, 1954). How the system worked day by day is charmingly told in *Sowing* (New York: Harcourt Brace Jovanovich, 1962), volume one of the autobiography of Leonard Woolf (Virginia Woolf's husband).
2. Alfred D. Chandler, Jr. has masterfully chronicled the process in his two books *Strategy and Structure* (Cambridge: MIT Press, 1962) and *The Visible Hand* (Cambridge: Harvard University Press, 1977)–surely the best studies of the administrative history of any major institution. The process itself and its results were presented and analyzed in two of my books: *The Concept of the Corporation* (New York: John Day, 1946) and *The Practice of Management* (New York: Harper Brothers, 1954).

Chapter 10

1. A good example is Myles Mace, "The President and the Board of Directors," *Harvard Business Review* 50, no. 2 (1972): 37.

Chapter 11

1. Among the few attempts to apply working smarter in health care are Roxanne Spitzer's *Nursing Productivity: The Hospital's Key to Survival and Profit* (Chicago: S-N Publications, 1986) and Regina Herzlinger's

Creating New Health Care Ventures (Gaithersburg, Md.: Aspen Publishers, 1991).

2. See Michael Hammer, "Reengineering Work: Don't Automate, Obliterate," *Harvard Business Review* 68, no. 4 (1990): 104–112; and Peter F. Drucker, "Permanent Cost Cutting," *Wall Street Journal,* 11 January 1991.

3. See Boris Emmet and John E. Jeucks, *Catalogues and Counters: A History of Sears, Roebuck & Company* (Chicago: University of Chicago Press, 1965).

4. In my 1942 book, *The Future of Industrial Man* (Westport, Conn.: Greenwood, 1978 reprint of original), and my 1950 book, *The New Society* (Greenwood, 1982 reprint), I argued for the "responsible worker" as "part of management." Edwards W. Deming and Joseph M. Juran developed what we now call "quality circles" and "total quality management" as a result of their wartime experiences. Finally, the idea was forcefully presented by Douglas McGregor in his 1960 book, *The Human Side of Enterprise* (New York: McGraw Hill, 1985, twenty-fifth anniversary printing), with its "Theory X" and "Theory Y."

Chapter 12

1. Robert Kaplan, "Yesterday's Accounting Undermines Production," *Harvard Business Review* 62, no. 4 (1984): 95–101.

Index

About the Author

Peter Drucker on the Profession of Management marks the publication of Peter Drucker's thirtieth book. Of the preceding twenty-nine—the first one published in 1939–thirteen deal with management, thirteen deal with society, economics, and politics, two are novels, and one is autobiographical.

In addition, Mr. Drucker has published more than thirty articles in the *Harvard Business Review*. Several of these articles have received McKinsey Awards. He has been a frequent contributor to magazines such as *The Atlantic Monthly* and was a columnist for the *Wall Street Journal* from 1975 to 1995.

Mr. Drucker's first consulting assignment was in 1940. Since then he has consulted widely–in the United States, Europe, Latin America, and Asia–with large and small businesses, government agencies, and non-profit organizations. He is the Honorary Chairman of the Peter F. Drucker Foundation for Nonprofit Management.

After teaching at Sarah Lawrence College in New York from 1939 to 1942 and at Bennington College in Vermont from 1942 to 1949, Mr. Drucker became a professor of management at the Graduate Business School of New York University in 1950. In 1971 he became the Clarke Professor of Social Science & Management at the Graduate Management School of Claremont University, where he still teaches today. In 1987, Claremont University named its graduate management school in honor of him. Mr. Drucker holds honorary doctorates from universities in the United States, Belgium, the Czech Republic, Japan, Spain, Switzerland, and the United Kingdom.